The Culture of Beauty

Other Books of Related Interest:

At Issue Series

Beauty Pageants

Current Controversies Series

Human Genetics

Introducing Issues with Opposing Viewpoints Series

Self-Mutilation

Issues That Concern You Series

Eating Disorders

Opposing Viewpoints Series

The Culture of Beauty

The Fashion Industry

Health

The Culture of Beauty

Laurie Willis, Book Editor

GREENHAVEN PRESS
A part of Gale, Cengage Learning

Detroit • New York • San Francisco • New Haven, Conn • Waterville, Maine • London

Christine Nasso, *Publisher*
Elizabeth Des Chenes, *Managing Editor*

For more information, contact:
Greenhaven Press
27500 Drake Rd.
Farmington Hills, MI 48331-3535
Or you can visit our Internet site at gale.cengage.com

Articles in Greenhaven Press anthologies are often edited for length to meet page requirements. In addition, original titles of these works are changed to clearly present the main thesis and to explicitly indicate the author's opinion. Every effort is made to ensure that Greenhaven Press accurately reflects the original intent of the authors. Every effort has been made to trace the owners of copyrighted material.

LIBRARY OF CONGRESS CATALOGING-IN-PUBLICATION DATA

The culture of beauty / Laurie Willis, book editor.
p. cm. -- (Global viewpoints)
Includes bibliographical references and index.
ISBN 978-0-7377-4929-8 (hardcover) -- ISBN 978-0-7377-4930-4 (pbk.)
1. Beauty, Personal. 2. Beauty culture. 3. Body image in women. 4. Human body--Social aspects. I. Willis, Laurie.
GT499.C85 2010
646.7--dc22

2010018201

Printed in the United States of America
2 3 4 5 6 7 14 13 12 11

Contents

Chapter 3: Enhancing the Body

Chapter 4: Ethnic and Religious Dress

Foreword

> *"The problems of all of humanity can only be solved by all of humanity."*
> *—Swiss author Friedrich Dürrenmatt*

Global interdependence has become an undeniable reality. Mass media and technology have increased worldwide access to information and created a society of global citizens. Understanding and navigating this global community is a challenge, requiring a high degree of information literacy and a new level of learning sophistication.

Building on the success of its flagship series, *Opposing Viewpoints*, Greenhaven Press has created the *Global Viewpoints* series to examine a broad range of current, often controversial topics of worldwide importance from a variety of international perspectives. Providing students and other readers with the information they need to explore global connections and think critically about worldwide implications, each *Global Viewpoints* volume offers a panoramic view of a topic of widespread significance.

Drugs, famine, immigration—a broad, international treatment is essential to do justice to social, environmental, health, and political issues such as these. Junior high, high school, and early college students, as well as general readers, can all use *Global Viewpoints* anthologies to discern the complexities relating to each issue. Readers will be able to examine unique national perspectives while, at the same time, appreciating the interconnectedness that global priorities bring to all nations and cultures.

Material in each volume is selected from a diverse range of sources, including journals, magazines, newspapers, nonfiction books, speeches, government documents, pamphlets, organization newsletters, and position papers. *Global Viewpoints* is truly global, with material drawn primarily from international sources available in English and secondarily from U.S. sources with extensive international coverage.

Features of each volume in the *Global Viewpoints* series include:

- An **annotated table of contents** that provides a brief summary of each essay in the volume, including the name of the country or area covered in the essay.
- An **introduction** specific to the volume topic.
- A **world map** to help readers locate the countries or areas covered in the essays.
- For each viewpoint, an **introduction** that contains notes about the author and source of the viewpoint explains why material from the specific country is being presented, summarizes the main points of the viewpoint, and offers three **guided reading questions** to aid in understanding and comprehension.
- **For further discussion** questions that promote critical thinking by asking the reader to compare and contrast aspects of the viewpoints or draw conclusions about perspectives and arguments.
- A worldwide list of **organizations to contact** for readers seeking additional information.
- A **periodical bibliography** for each chapter and a **bibliography of books** on the volume topic to aid in further research.
- A comprehensive **subject index** to offer access to people, places, events, and subjects cited in the text, with the countries covered in the viewpoints highlighted.

Global Viewpoints is designed for a broad spectrum of readers who want to learn more about current events, history, political science, government, international relations, economics, environmental science, world cultures, and sociology—students doing research for class assignments or debates, teachers and faculty seeking to supplement course materials, and others wanting to understand current issues better. By presenting how people in various countries perceive the root causes, current consequences, and proposed solutions to worldwide challenges, *Global Viewpoints* volumes offer readers opportunities to enhance their global awareness and their knowledge of cultures worldwide.

Introduction

> *"There is certainly no absolute standard of beauty. That precisely is what makes its pursuit so interesting."*
>
> *John Kenneth Galbraith, Canadian American economist*

Although there will never be one consistent standard of beauty throughout the world, and by all accounts nor should there be, there is a common desire throughout various cultures to adorn oneself for important occasions. The following quote from the book *Dress and Adornment*, by Peter Magubane and Sandra Klopper, is about tribal culture in Africa, but with a little rephrasing it could just as well apply to people anywhere in the world:

> Extravagant clothing and adornments are commonly adopted on special occasions such as weddings, the installation of chiefs, celebrations commemorating cultural and other heroes, the coming-out ceremonies of young women, and the joyous reception by friends and family members of pre- and post-pubescent male and female initiates following their return to their communities. This practice stems from a desire to give expression to particular social, political, or religious values.

Celebrations of all kinds—holidays, parties, weddings, religious ceremonies, etc.—evoke the human tendency to want to look one's best, to put one's "best self" forward.

Taking time to dress carefully, apply makeup and style hair enhances anticipation and is a way to honor the importance of the occasion, serving as a reminder that this particular event is set apart from normal day-to-day activities. In her

book *The Beauty Industry: Gender, Culture, Pleasure,* Paula Black explains how this is apparent in some beauty salons in the United Kingdom (UK):

> Weddings in the UK among people of South Asian origin are elaborate and highly significant. An important part of the preparation for the bride and members of the two families is to undergo beauty treatments. Much of the business among salons catering to a South Asian clientele comes from weddings. Holidays lead to an increase in body hair waxing and other preparations which either alter appearance for this special occasion or save the woman time from routine bodily maintenance tasks while away from home. Holidays serve an important function in management of appearance where the woman is herself but more so. New styles may be tested out and space is provided to experiment with body image. The purchase and packing of clothes and toiletries is, therefore, a vital aspect of holidays, as are the preparations undertaken in the beauty salon.

Cultures across the world approach preparations for festive occasions in different ways. The Africans that Magubane and Klopper describe don't need money, but use natural materials that are readily available, such as pieces of vegetation and dyes made from plants, and prepare their own designs or help decorate one another. An American bride, on the other hand, might spend hours shopping and thousands of dollars on a designer dress, makeup, and beauty treatments.

In many places, what is considered beautiful has changed dramatically in recent years. Due to globalization (the increased integration and exchange of ideas and goods globally) styles from Western cultures are being worn all over the world. In some countries, many people wear westernized clothing in daily life, reserving more traditional ethnic dress (for example, a sari or kimono) for special events. In *Wedding Dress Across Cultures,* edited by Helen Bradley Foster and Donald Clay Johnson, Masami Suga describes a typical contemporary Japanese bridal costume. The dress is a modernization of the traditional kimono, which is seldom worn except on special occasions:

> A bride almost always wears a wedding kimono with a headdress. Today's style combines a hair wig and a headdress into one. The wig replicates the earlier hairstyle created with a bride's own hair when the kimono was the everyday fashion in Japan. The wig is decorated with ornamental hairpins and a *tsunokakushi* (literally, a horn-hider, representing the hiding of a bride's horns of jealousy) or a *watabóshi* (literally, a cotton-hat, which when worn covers a bride's head except for her face). Although modern Japanese women no longer wear kimonos on a daily basis, when worn, it is important to look properly coordinated from head to toe.

In other areas of the world, such as the highlands of Ecuador, traditional ethnic clothing is worn on ordinary days but westernized styles are worn at weddings and baptisms. Some traditional clothing is not worn at all by natives, but manufactured for sale to the tourist industry. For example, according to Anne P. Rowe and Lynne Meisch in their book, *Costume and Identity in Highland Ecuador*, one style of men's shirt "is no longer commonly worn by indigenous men, but has evolved into a tourist item and is sold in the market as the 'Otavalo wedding shirt.'"

As evidenced in this brief look at dress for special occasions, ideas of style and beauty vary widely. *Global Viewpoints: The Culture of Beauty* explores ideals of beauty from around the world through a variety of perspectives. The first chapter highlights some definitions and standards of beauty in different parts of the world. Chapter two gives several perspectives on body image—the way people feel about their own bodies and how they envision the ideal beautiful body, which varies from culture to culture. The third chapter discusses various ways people enhance their bodies, from makeup to plastic surgery, to tattoos and scarification. The final chapter explores

the views of several different cultures on fashion and clothing. Taken together, the viewpoints present a vast array of beauty ideals throughout the world.

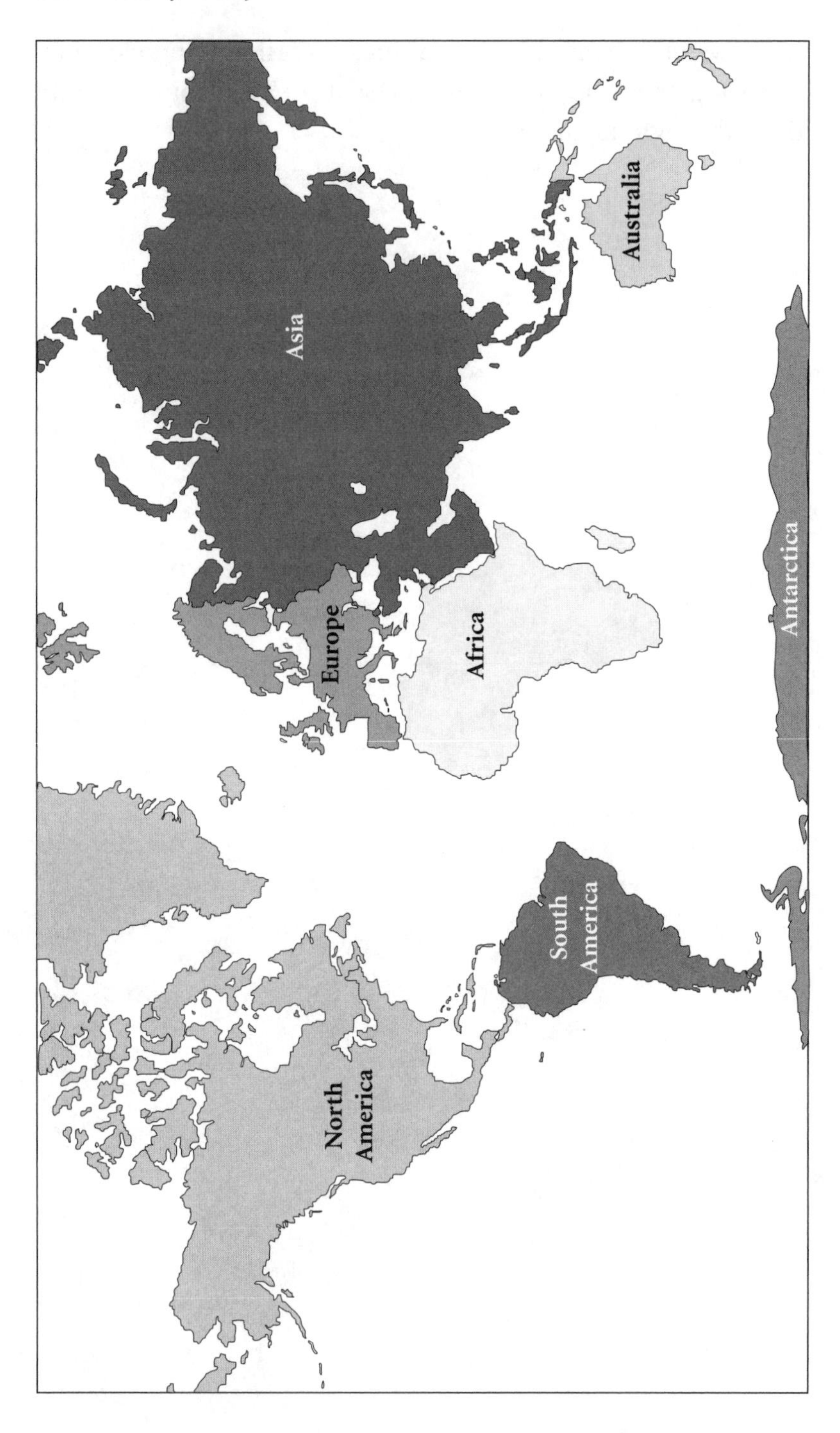
Asia
Australia
Europe
Africa
Antarctica
South America
North America

CHAPTER 1

Global Definitions of Beauty

Viewpoint 1

Throughout History, Ideals of Beauty Have Not Been Universal

Lars Svendsen

Lars Svendsen is a professor of philosophy at the University of Norway. In the following excerpt from his book, Fashion: A Philosophy, *Svendsen takes a philosophical look at the concept of beauty and concludes that there are no universal ideals of beauty, but rather ideals of beauty are relative, dependent on time and place.*

As you read, consider the following questions:

1. What percentage of men in the United States does Svendsen say are dissatisfied with their appearances?
2. According to fashion theorist Valerie Steele, what has happened in the evolution of corsets?
3. What invention does Svendsen say made it sensible for women to wear trousers?

If life really is a beauty competition, as the fashion designer Thierry Mugler has claimed, one must hope to have been born at a time when the norms of beauty happen to correspond to one's natural features. According to Robert Musil:

> There are, of course, in all periods all kinds of countenances, but only one type will be singled by a period's taste

Lars Svendsen, *Fashion: A Philosophy*, translated by John Irons, London, United Kingdom: Reaktion, 2006, pp. 80–89.

as its ideal image of happiness and beauty while all the other faces do their best to copy it, and with the help of fashion and hairdressers even the ugly ones manage to approximate the ideal. But there are some faces that never succeed, faces born to a strange distinction of their own, unyieldingly expressing the regal and banished ideal beauty of an earlier period.

We live in an age, however, when the unhappy souls born with the ideal of beauty of another age have a greater opportunity than ever before of being able to fit in with their own age. There are limits to how much a body can be modified via cosmetics, hairstyles and training, but by intervening more directly via cosmetic surgery (removing a little here and adding a little there) the ideal of beauty that applies at any given time can apparently be brought within the reach of more and more people.

The hours spent in the gym and the intervention of the plastic surgeon are not seen as imposed on the individual from outside. Apparently, one freely chooses to replace fat by muscle and to submit to the surgeon's scalpel.

The Rise in Popularity of Cosmetic Surgery

Cosmetic surgery is mushrooming as an industry. Even in Norway, a country with a population of about 4.6 million, it was estimated in 2004 that about 80,000 Norwegian women have undergone cosmetic surgery and about 250,000 more say that they are contemplating it. That is far from 'all women', but it is a considerable number, one that is rising sharply from year to year. This is not just affecting women, either. Karl Kraus's aphorism that 'Cosmetics is the study of the female cosmos' has become increasingly applicable to men. Today's man is placed in a world where his external appearance, towards which he has a reflective attitude, is becoming of crucial importance to how he views himself. One recent study claims that 43 per cent of all men in the US [United States] are dissatisfied with their appearance—three times as many as 25 years ago. More and more men are modifying their appearance by cosmetic surgery.

We have definitely seen a normalization of cosmetic surgery, which enables an adaptation to a norm over and above what can be achieved by the body's own work on itself. A fascinating case in this connection is the French performance artist Orlan, whose work is herself. From 1990 she was engaged on the *Reincarnation of Saint Orlan*, which required her to undergo a series of plastic surgery operations and thereby recreate herself using features taken from works of art, such as the chin from [Sandro] Botticelli's *[The Birth of] Venus* and the eyes of [François] Boucher's *[The Rape of] Europa*. Most people who undergo cosmetic surgery do so with far less radical intent, but the basic principle is the same—to reform the body to correspond to a given ideal. Cosmetic surgery is only a radicalization of earlier forms of body modification: There is only a difference of degree between having a haircut and having liposuction or a silicone implant. Other forms of body modification, such as piercing, tattooing and scar decoration, also became highly popular in the 1990s. Like all other fashions, however, the trend died away when the fashion became too widespread. Tattoos, however, are a paradoxical fashion phenomenon. Their relative permanence ought initially to make them rather ill-suited as a fashion, since it is not possible simply to get rid of them when the fashion is over. This brings us to an interesting point. Various forms of body decoration (from makeup to more radical body modifications) are found in all cultures, but generally speaking these play a group-identifying role in non-Western societies. In our modern Western societies, however, they are on the contrary interpreted as an assertion of individuality.

Pursuing an Ideal Body

According to Harold Koda, a curator at the Metropolitan Museum of Art: 'Fashion is the evidence of the human impulse to bring the body closer to an elusive transient ideal'. As the fashion theorist Valerie Steele has remarked, the corset never really disappeared; it was rather converted into other types of underwear and finally into the well-trained modern body. Jean Paul Gaultier's corsets, which were to be worn on top of the clothes rather than underneath them, were a clear comment on this. The hard shapes of the corset were no longer to keep human fat in—and the hard surface was rather just an expression of a body that had become hard. Is one free of the corset when one no longer shapes the body by means of it and has shaped it instead by realizing the same norm via endless hours in a keep-fit studio or gym? The hours spent in the gym and the intervention of the plastic surgeon are not seen as imposed on the individual from the outside. Apparently, one freely chooses to replace fat by muscle and to submit to the surgeon's scalpel. At the same time it is obvious that this free choice is not unqualified at all but takes place on the basis of an internalization of social norms.

[Jean] Baudrillard writes: 'Like dieting, bodybuilding, and so many other things, jogging is a new form of voluntary servitude'. The disciplinary power that most people are affected by is not that exercised behind prison walls, but is that exerted via television, newspapers, magazines and the media, which present us with an ideal for the physical self that will always be out of reach for almost everybody. The body becomes something that will always fall short. The ideal constantly changes, usually becoming more extreme, so that anyone who happens to achieve a body ideal will soon have fallen short of the next one. Even models fall short of the norms: As far back as the 1950s it was not unusual for some to undergo cosmetic surgery in order to approach the norm, for example by removing the back molars in order to achieve hollow cheeks, or by having ribs removed in order to get the right body shape. The discrepancy between models' bodies and 'normal' bodies continues to increase. Today, the average American model weighs 23 per cent less than the average American woman, whereas only a generation ago the difference was 8 per cent. The models are closest to the norm, but even their bodies, which are quite extreme to start with, are further modified by computerized image manipulation. In this way, the norm becomes pure fiction, but does not lose its normative function because of that.

Changing Concepts of 'Natural'

The sociologist Anthony Giddens draws attention to how the body is becoming increasingly 'reflexively mobilised', that rather than being something 'given', it is subjected to 'fashioning' work. All physical skills such as walking, smiling and swimming are technical and social. Walking is not purely instinctive and value-neutral in human beings—it is learned in a social field and expresses different values. There is a considerable difference between the gait of a slacker and a regular officer. The way one walks is socially formed, and there is no completely 'natural' way of walking, even though some certainly seem to be more exaggerated than others. Not only is the body saturated in social norms when in activity, it is so at rest as well.

With the exception of extreme practices such as feet-binding, we can hardly claim that one fashion is more 'natural' than another, since what can be seen as 'natural' is just as changeable as fashion itself. When we look at portraits of women from the late medieval period they often seem bizarre, to put it mildly. They have a very short, slim upper body topped by a large head and then, beneath two tiny breasts, there is an amply curved, though fairly unshapely, lower body that almost looks like some huge plinth [a square block serving as the base of a structure] for the small upper body. But that seemed 'natural' to people at the time. The late Gothic period's swelling bellies seem strange to us, and in the latter sixteenth century there would seem to be no limits as to how large a stomach a woman could have and yet still be attractive. On the contrary, it would seem that the norm was the bigger the better. It must be pointed out, however, that a toned 'hard body' from the 1980s would have seemed weird to someone from the late Gothic period. In the early seventeenth century [painter Peter Paul] Rubens would hardly have been impressed by Kate Moss's body, and the typical Rubens model would never be let loose on a catwalk nowadays, as presumably she would be at least ten sizes too big. One ideal of beauty that is quite unique to our age is visible bones. A constant feature of all ideals of beauty until the First World War was that a beautiful body had to have enough fat and muscle for the skeleton to remain hidden beneath them. Visible ribs and hips were 'unnatural' and ugly. The ideology of beauty normally operates with an idea of something 'natural', but the 'natural' body is, historically and socially speaking, an extremely variable entity. It must be pointed out that there have also been periods, such as during the later seventeenth century and the eighteenth, when the 'artificial' was approved fashion, but the crucial thing is that both 'natural' and 'artificial' ideals are constructs that change over time.

'Nature' has never been a guide when it comes to ideal bodies, even though each age has a tendency to regard its own ideal as being 'the natural'. What is a 'natural' position for the waist? In the seventeenth century the waist moved down to what we now regard its 'natural' position, but it has moved up and down quite a lot since then. Even if we confine ourselves to the twentieth century, we can see that it has moved between the hips and the breasts. Where the 'natural' position of the waist is would seem to be something that is completely a matter of convention. Changes in ideal bodies can be seen from display dummies. In the early twentieth century they had relatively strong shoulders and upper arms while the waist was slender (the classic hourglass figure), with breasts protruding forwards and posterior backwards. Dummies [mannequins] of the 1920s, on the other hand, are characterized by a much slimmer figure, although collar bones or distinct muscles are not visible until the 1930s, which had a slimmer ideal body than any previous time in history. After the Second World War breasts and hips become larger again, whereas those of the 1960s have a more androgynous and angular figure. In the 1970s the most important development is that the dummies also display features of people from other parts of the world, but even so the ideal remains slim and youthful—a trend that has lasted until the present day. It should also be pointed out that not only the female body has been subject to the cultural conventions that prevail at any given time and adjust the relationships between the various parts of the body. Men too have had to adapt to the prevailing norms, for example by wearing a corset, but the results have normally been less radical than demanded of women. The ideals for the male body have mainly been linked to the size of the shoulders, hips and stomach. There has normally been a connection between the ideal bodies for both sexes, with a generous stomach or a slim waist being the approved norm for both sexes at the same time. When breasts are emphasized in women, however, the tendency has been for men's shoulders to become broader.

Are there 'natural' reasons for men and women wearing different clothes? Before the fourteenth century the differences between clothing for men and women are relatively small, but after that point the shape of clothes tends to be related to gender, with women wearing dresses that were admittedly more body-hugging than clothes worn previously, while men began to wear tights with short trousers worn over them. The idea that men's and women's bodies are basically similar, but that a woman's body—especially the genitals—is less developed than a man's, was not abandoned until the seventeenth century. In the course of the following century, however, it became increasingly usual to consider men and women as basically different with regard to both physical and mental characteristics. The philosopher Jean-Jacques Rousseau is a typical example of this way of thinking. Men's and women's fashions also became correspondingly divergent. What is cause and what is effect, to what extent changes in the view of gender influenced fashion, or vice versa, is difficult to decide. It is most likely that the changes in clothes fashions and the view of gender tended to reinforce each other.

If one searches for universal ideals of beauty, one is liable to emerge empty-handed.

Trousers are a good example of what Roland Barthes calls a 'mythologization' (i.e., naturalization), by which a completely contingent definition is raised to the status of a natural law. There is no physiological reason for trousers being a specifically male garment. In nineteenth-century France women were actually forbidden to wear trousers, although working-class women in particular broke this prohibition. Knickers were also highly suspect, as the separation of a woman's thighs, even by a small piece of fabric, was considered directly obscene. Girls could wear knickers until puberty, but not subsequently, as the only adult women who wore them were prostitutes. Various attempts to introduce knickers were made in the mid-nineteenth century. American feminists were among those who began to wear loose pantaloons gathered at the ankle, known as bloomers. These were named after Amelia Bloomer, who designed and wore them in public about 1850. The pioneers were forced to abandon the attempt because they were ridiculed to such an extent that they became a liability to the American feminist movement. The invention and spread of the bicycle, however, which was well established by the 1890s,

Beauty Ideals Relate to Cultural Values

Ideals relate to the cultural values that exist in a society. When applied to dress, these values connect to those physical characteristics prized by people at a particular point in time and place. Thus, sometimes a sturdy woman's figure has been considered more desirable than a slim one, for a sturdy body represents good health and the ability to undertake hard work and bear many children. For example, among Munda agriculturalists in central India, a family might send their daughter out to bring buckets of water from the well to show off her strength to the parents of a prospective bridegroom. A highly desirable muscular-armed bride can carry one in each hand and a third on her head. In contrast, good health may easily be taken for granted where medical technology is advanced and accessible. Physical labor and childbearing are not as relevant in North America and Europe for marriageability where many people work in service and white-collar jobs and admire small family size.

Joanne B. Eicher, Sandra Lee Evenson, and Hazel A. Lutz, The Visible Self: Global Perspectives on Dress, Culture, and Society. *New York: Fairchild Publications, Inc., 2008, p. 337.*

made it sensible for women to wear trousers, since it was highly impractical to cycle wearing a skirt. At first a kind of divided skirt was worn, but gradually this gave way to normal trousers. From the 1920s and '30s it became more usual for women to wear trousers (both long and short) for sport and leisure activities. Yet, even so, several decades were to pass before a woman wearing trousers could go to the office or to a party without attracting negative attention.

Body Preferences Change over Time

Once women began to show their legs in the twentieth century these became the most erotic part of the body. There are considerable historical variations when it comes to which part of the body is considered particularly attractive, this being reflected in their being emphasized or covered by clothes. There are also variations when it comes to what skin colour is considered attractive. Before the 1920s a brown skin colour was thought vulgar by prosperous white people, because this colour was linked to physical labour in the sun. In the 1920s, however, rich Americans began to take their holidays on the French Riviera, and it soon became fashionable to be tanned. Over the past few decades a strong tan has become somewhat less fashionable, perhaps because 'everybody' could now afford holidays down south, perhaps following health scares. Generally speaking, though, it is now difficult to say that any particular skin colour is the single norm.

A part of the body that has undergone interesting transformations in the name of fashion is the female breast. It was not until the mid-fifteenth century that clothes were developed that made it obvious that women actually have breasts and partially drew attention to this fact, although it was well disguised. Two centuries were to pass before full breasts were presented as attractive. Before that time large breasts were thought of as common and vulgar—absolutely not something for the higher echelons of society, which was normative. Ideal breasts became larger during the seventeenth century before decreasing once more in the eighteenth century, assuming an apple-like shape that was retained as the standard until the end of the nineteenth century, when ideal breasts once more became fuller and more central for 'femininity'. The ideal size of breasts varied considerably during the twentieth century. It is remarkable how little the development of the ideal breast has corresponded to the ideal body in general. The 'natural' thing would be for a slender body to have small breasts and an ampler ideal body to have large breasts, since despite everything there is a certain correlation between the size of breasts and the amount of body fat elsewhere. But the exact opposite would seem to have been the case: Ample bodies have had small breasts and slim bodies have had relatively large breasts—as is the case today.

What is 'beautiful', what would represent a deviation from a beauty norm and what role such a deviation plays are all relative when it comes to time and place. If one searches for universal ideals of beauty, one is liable to emerge empty-handed. Apart from symmetrical features having been, generally speaking, considered attractive and asymmetrical ones the opposite, it is very difficult to find any universal 'beautiful' qualities. Symmetry can be found in many variants: both slender and ample bodies can be symmetrical, small and large eyes, long and short legs, narrow and wide shoulders. Even so, symmetry is generally a central feature. Not least because of this [Japanese fashion designer] Rei Kawakubo's experiments with asymmetrical shapes have been thought-provoking. These items rewrite the body, and she is reported as saying that in her work 'the body becomes dress becomes body'. The human figure when wearing these clothes looks distorted, and yet beautiful, so that Kawakubo would thereby seem to be questioning symmetry as a necessary ingredient of the ideal of beauty. Kawakubo creates clothes that seem 'unnatural' to a Western gaze, because they have not been created in accordance with Western conventions, but this also makes clear to what extent our way of looking is determined by these conventions, since we see that they could have been different.

VIEWPOINT 2

Western Ideals of Physical Beauty

Arthur Marwick

Arthur Marwick was a professor of history who taught at several universities in Great Britain, France, and the United States. In his book, IT: A History of Human Beauty, *he argues that ideals of beauty in Western cultures have remained relatively the same over time, but the way that beauty is valued has changed. The following viewpoint is excerpted from the first chapter of his book, in which he puts forth the theories that he elaborates on in the remainder of the work.*

As you read, consider the following questions:

1. According to a study quoted by Marwick, what is the financial penalty for being plain?
2. To what other genetic gifts does Marwick compare beauty?
3. List two disadvantages of being beautiful cited by Marwick.

As every doctor knows, people habitually overstate how often they're having sex while understating how much alcohol they drink. But of all human attributes, the one over which there is most dishonesty, most persistent refusal to face

Arthur Marwick, *IT: A History of Human Beauty*, London, United Kingdom: Hambledon and London, 2004, pp. 1–24.

the facts, most doublethink, is physical appearance. Much of this, of course, is in the cause of common civility and decency: far kinder to pour out the balm of gentle flattery than to fling the corrosive acid of honest judgment on, say, a pudgy nose, piggy eyes, and a receding chin, or a face and figure (I am speaking of males as well as females) which are nondescript, plain and utterly devoid of allure. Civilisation has always depended upon the observance of certain polite fictions, and nowhere is there a richer growth of such fictions than in regard to questions of human beauty. Partly this is because of the special resonances, and special ambiguities, of the very concept of 'beauty'; partly, it is because personal appearance is intimately bound up with the sense of self-worth, and, more critically, with sexuality, sexual attractiveness and sexual success. Look up the thousands of tomes and treatises on 'beauty' and you'll find that most of them deal with moral or aesthetic beauty, often representing the two as being inextricably intertwined, very few descending to the mundane topic of the physical appearance of human beings. This is because the eternal quest has been for a universal concept of beauty, one which will cover poems, paintings, symphonies, statues, sunsets and seascapes (natural and imagined), beautiful bodies and beautiful minds.

'Beauty' is itself such a 'beautiful' concept that the conviction is that it must connote something transcendental, something beyond human affairs, such as truth, purity, godliness, spirituality, 'the good' to the utmost degree. Outstanding physical beauty (in both males and females), the less privileged of us cannot help noting, offers its possessors sexual opportunity aplenty, and thus hints at promiscuity, lust and carnal gluttony—indulgences incompatible with any rarified notions of the meaning of beauty. For someone to be 'truly beautiful', the implication is, they must possess some moral or spiritual qualities beyond being 'merely beautiful'. They must be irradiated by, as it is often put, an 'inner light'—for 'beauty', as the oft-repeated, but seldom-examined cliché has it, 'is more than skin deep'. One might actually say of someone, 'He's a beautiful person, even though he's not very good-looking'.

Yet while much lip service is paid to the notion of the transcendental quality of beauty, the overwhelming evidence is that in our everyday lives we are actually obsessed by surface appearance, those enjoying great natural beauty always attracting special attention, sometimes adoration, sometimes hatred, there being frequent laments about the unfair advantages enjoyed by the comely and the cruel penalties imposed on the ugly. . . .

The eternal quest has been for a universal concept of beauty, one which will cover poems, paintings, symphonies, statues, sunsets and seascapes (natural and imagined), beautiful bodies and beautiful minds.

Ideas of Human Beauty Are Universal

My contention is that ideas of what, in the Western world, have constituted human beauty are more universal, and less subject to variation (though they have been subject to expansion and increasing flexibility), than is assumed, practically without reflection or examination, by trendy theory. What has changed though, and that is a central theme of this book, is the way in which beauty is *valued*. Today, the evidence lies all around us that our civilisation as it exists now has an intense preoccupation with personal appearance, and gives a very high rating to human beauty. Whether on the billboards which line our streets and stations, in the glossy magazines which jostle for position on bookstalls and in the newsagents, or during the regular assaults of the television commercials on our own living rooms, we see that the received method of marketing products of every type is to associate them with a beautiful human being, whether male or female. It is a commonplace that, as technology advanced in tandem with conflicts in Kosovo, Afghanistan, and Iraq, television also brought the heat of battle into our homes; at the same time one could not avoid noting that the new generation of war reporters were, to an astonishing degree, beautiful young women, with a scattering of beautiful young men, one of whom, Rageh Omaar, a black BBC reporter, was apparently so attractive to American females he acquired the nickname 'The Scud Stud'. Today, in a wide range of jobs, particularly those in any form of communications, the possession of personal beauty is an enormous asset. Nearly twenty years ago I made the case that human beauty in the late twentieth century was coming to assume an independent value of its own, rivalling such qualities as status, wealth and education, and being possessed, indeed, of considerable commercial value. Since then a number of hardheaded economic studies have conclusively demonstrated that in many areas the beautiful get the better jobs, pull in the higher earnings. Here, in prime Wall Street jargon, is the conclusion from the first of these studies:

> Holding constant demographic and labor-market characteristics, plain people earn less than people of average looks, who earn less than the good-looking. The penalty for plainness is 5 to 10 per cent, slightly larger than the premium for beauty. The effects are slightly larger for men than women; but unattractive women are less likely than others to participate in the labor force and are more likely to be married to men with unexpectedly low human capital. Better-looking people sort into occupations where beauty is likely to be more productive; but the impact of individuals' looks on their earnings is mostly independent of occupation.

Ironically, this utterly practical research, demonstrating that, with respect to fundamental earning power, beauty was certainly no myth, had in part been stimulated by the runaway best seller, *The Beauty Myth: How Images of Beauty Are Used Against Women* by Naomi Wolf (1990), which argued that ideals of female beauty were deliberately constructed by men in order to perpetuate their rule over women; by writing off large numbers of women as 'not beautiful' they could, Wolf claimed, keep these women in a permanent state of oppression. Like all spinners of absurd relativist theory, Wolf was obsessed by the notion that men are driven by the search for power, when most, in fact, are driven by the search for pleasure. Hence her ludicrous and (at that time) intellectually trendy contention that: 'The beauty myth is not about women at all. It is all about men and power'. If men actually could 'construct' female beauty, it would be in their interest not to restrict the amount of beauty but to create as much as possible, so that there would be plenty of lovely sex mates to go round. In any case, as the survey I have just quoted brings out, the bonus of beauty was now being enjoyed by men as well as women. Wolf was herself a very beautiful young woman, and looked terrific in her many television interviews. It is, of course, one of the benefits of that distinctly non-mythical attribute, beauty, that it can enable its possessors to get away with talking complete tripe.

The method of marketing products of every type is to associate them with a beautiful human being, whether male or female.

Beauty Is a Genetic Gift

No doubt it *is* unfair that some individuals are beautiful and most are not; but then it is also unfair that a relative minority have musical talent, mathematical talent, artistic talent, literary talent, acting talent, business talent, sporting talent, the uniquely flexible cartilages and joints which make possible the exquisite contortions of the ballet dancer. It's true that exploitation of the main range of human talents calls for dedication, training and hard work in a way that exploitation of beauty generally does not, though . . . the exploitation of beauty usu-

Combining Spiritual and Physical Beauty

Attempts to articulate the nature and value of beauty can be divided into two basic types. On the one hand, we may concentrate on the fact that beauty is something apprehended in perception—beauty is something we can see or hear: It is rhythm, line, shape, structure. . . . On the other hand, we may concentrate on the spiritual or moral aspects of the encounter with beauty; hence we might be tempted to say that beauty is truth; or the promise of happiness, or the intimation of moral perfection. Such suggestions hint at the power of beauty. . . . If the two tendencies are so well established it is perhaps because each, in its own way, is correct. The fuller grasp of beauty does not require us to decide which is right and to abandon the other approach. Rather, it requires that we see how the two are connected.

The experience of beauty, we may then say, consists in finding a spiritual value (truth, happiness, moral ideals) at home in a material setting (rhythm, line, shape, structure) and in such a way that, while we contemplate the object, the two seem inseparable. To be human is to experience life under two guises: physical and spiritual—this is how it seems, whatever the underlying facts. Thus the experience of beauty is a reflection, as it were, of what it is to be human. Not in the ordinary times, when we feel divided or dissatisfied, but in the moments of deepest satisfaction. And while our best moments are passing and irrecoverable, the beautiful object is permanently available, waiting for our love.

John Armstrong, The Secret Power of Beauty. *London: Penguin Books, 2004, p. 162–163.*

ally does call for elements of thought, patience, strategy and, often, the exercise of another talent or talents. But whether we are talking of the most formidable intellect, the most sublime artistic genius, or merely great natural beauty, each is, ultimately, a gift from the genes. In the past the beautiful cashed in on their looks almost exclusively by granting sexual favours to the powerful. But in modern mass democratic society, though beauty, of course, continues to carry its elemental sexual charge, its commercial value, based on its appeal to masses of people, as consumers, viewers, audiences, no longer depends on sexual transactions (though jobs putting sexuality up for sale continue to blossom—from male prostitution to female lap dancing). The advantages conferred by beauty can be irritating, even infuriating. But try this simple test: Would you really prefer there to be fewer (perhaps even no) beautiful people in the world, or more of them? Most of us recognise that, in fact, we get immense pleasure from the company of beautiful people (of both sexes), from beholding them, and (generally) experience a sense of lift when a beautiful person comes into the room; and that, short of getting what we really want (a stunningly beautiful sex mate for our ourselves) we would rather have more of the beautiful around than fewer of them. Thus, while I am not going to equate the possession of perfect form and features to the talent of a Luciano Pavarotti, or a Bill Gates, I do maintain that that particular and very specific gift does enrich the lives of others. What causes the agony is the mad pursuit of beauty when it is better to recognise that, like the vast majority, we do not possess it, and the failure to recognise that there are so many other worthwhile personal qualities, such as friendliness, generosity and understanding.

That beauty is fascinating, disturbing, intensely real (in other words no myth) is apparent from the (highly rational) attention it is receiving from the post-feminist generation.

Ellen Zetzel Lambert in *The Face of Love: Feminism and the Beauty Question* (1995) poses the questions:

> What is the nature of the elusive but surely real relationship between a person's outward appearance and his or her inner nature? Why should some people seem so beautiful to us on a first meeting, then not so beautiful as we come to know them better, while the beauty of others reveals itself to us only over time?

My fundamental point is that beauty is no figment, no myth: beauty exists. It stands out, it arouses desire, it is disturbing; it may bring success or it may bring tragedy.

[Author] Wendy Steiner . . . has advised that instead of giving themselves eating disorders in the pursuit of perfect beauty, which, unlike many earlier feminists of a post-modernist persuasion, she clearly accepts does actually exist, women should 'see themselves as beautiful in a more human sense—valuable, worthy of love.' This echoes the advice advanced fifteen years earlier by Nancy C. Baker in her *The Beauty Trap: How Every Woman Can Free Herself from It*—and, indeed, that of wise post-feminist women everywhere:

> Isn't it time that we redefined beauty for ourselves so that it includes far more than perfect features, artfully enhanced makeup, hairstyling and clothing. My own new definition, for instance, is that a truly beautiful woman makes the best of her physical assets but, more important, she also *radiates a personal quality which is attractive.* Unlike the woman with a gorgeous face and body who is obsessed with herself, my ideally beautiful woman exudes concern for others, as well as intelligence, enthusiasm, humour, and self-confidence. These are all qualities we can cultivate in ourselves, and they're qualities that will last us a lifetime.

Physical Beauty Is Separate from Other Positive Qualities

Sensible as these arguments are for the everyday living of life, they simply take us back to the subterfuges discussed at the beginning of this chapter, blurring the distinction between being physically beautiful (having 'a gorgeous face and body'—don't we need to preserve the obvious word for that rare and disturbing condition?) and being 'nice', 'human', 'considerate'. The curious point about these feminist and post-feminist works is that, while I have always been concerned with the implications of beauty in men as well as of beauty in women (though my feminist critics refused to give me any credit for this), they are exclusively concerned with looks in women. This book deals equally with 'the man with the gorgeous face and body'. I regret Baker's slander that the beautiful woman is necessarily 'obsessed with herself': Many beautiful women are 'considerate' and 'human'—feminists ruin their own arguments when they suggest otherwise. Actually, I will be showing that, historically, gorgeous men (unlike most gorgeous women) have tended to be rather stupidly 'obsessed with themselves'.

My fundamental point is that beauty is no figment, no myth: Beauty exists. It stands out, it arouses desire, it is disturbing; it may bring success, or it may bring tragedy. As two women psychologists, Elaine Hatfield and Susan Sprecher, have put it their brilliant synthesis based on masses of empirical work, *Mirror, Mirror: The Importance of Looks in Everyday Life*:

> Undoubtedly, it is good to be good-looking when it comes to developing and maintaining personal relationships. Those possessed with good looks seem to have many advantages in their social lives . . . people do desire the company of attractive men and women. In most people's fantasies, the 'romantic other' is someone who looks like he/she just stepped out of the pages of *Glamour* magazine. When men and

> women do not have to worry about the possibility of being rejected, they tend to prefer the most attractive partner possible . . . attractiveness can stimulate passion—the best aphrodisiac seems to be an attractive partner.

Disadvantages of Beauty

Hatfield and Sprecher point out some of the disadvantages beauty can have (Paul Newman, whom they do not mention, was not alone among beautiful males in complaining that constant reference to his blue eyes distracted attention from his achievements as a highly intelligent actor and director—personally I doubt whether such compliments to a man or a woman, or the ones to [a] woman that feminists used to call 'demeaning': 'lovely face', 'nice legs', 'good body', 'stunning looks', etc., really are much of a burden.) Hatfield and Sprecher quote this from a 'beautiful' (their word) woman:

> I am small and blonde. Many men assume even before they've met me, that I am interested in romance. When men I don't even know start up with me, I get nonresponsive and irritable. I know what it will lead to. It's embarrassing. It's exhausting. No one will take no for an answer. I'm tired of saying no, again, and again, ever so politely.

To demonstrate that beautiful men suffer in the same way, Hatfield and Sprecher cite the case of a beautiful male journalist, Pat Jordan, who, in June 1982, published an article in *Mademoiselle*, entitled 'Confessions of a Handsome Devil':

> Everyone has fleeting sexual fantasies about one another. For some, however, these fantasies are not enough. When Jordan is not interested, some women feel betrayed and strike out. Friendship is not enough for them. Many beautiful women, attracted to him because of his looks, turned on him when he failed to respond.

No doubt Jordan was the source for this account, but Hatfield and Sprecher authenticate it by presenting it in their own words.

Beauty as aphrodisiac and provoker of sexual fantasy, as well as beauty as enhancement of earning power: These are the blunt, unambiguous ways in which beauty is evaluated today. But throughout the centuries, up until very recently, beauty, while always perceived as exceptional, and therefore as exciting and disturbing, was thoroughly enveloped in ambivalence and confusion. These have their origins in the nature of early—basically agricultural and land-owning—society, its customs and superstitions, and in the more self-conscious programmes and codes worked out by the ancient Greeks, then developed within the early Christian church.

VIEWPOINT 3

African Standards of Beauty

Nakedi Ribane

In this viewpoint, South African actress and model Nakedi Ribane discusses beauty from a black African perspective. She talks about the distinctive shape of the ideal African woman's body, and how that shape differs from the thinner white ideal. In addition, she discusses how cosmetics, beauty pageants, and the modeling industry are influencing young African girls.

As you read, consider the following questions:

1. How does Ribane describe traditional African beauty?
2. What does Ribane say about the future of beauty contests?
3. According to the author, what happened with Roaccutane, a drug for patients with acne?

Is there such a thing as an ideal African beauty standard? What constitutes a beautiful woman in African terms and what are the characteristics that have traditionally been prized? Although these things have not been formally documented, they are well known within communities and have been passed down from generation to generation in the form of popular songs and folklore. Just as in the West, Africans had their own 'legendary' beauties who took centre stage in their communities. They are immortalised in traditional tales and songs and

Nakedi Ribane, *Beauty: A Black Perspective*, Scottsville, South Africa: University of KwaZulu-Natal Press, 2006, pp. 19–20, 122–126.

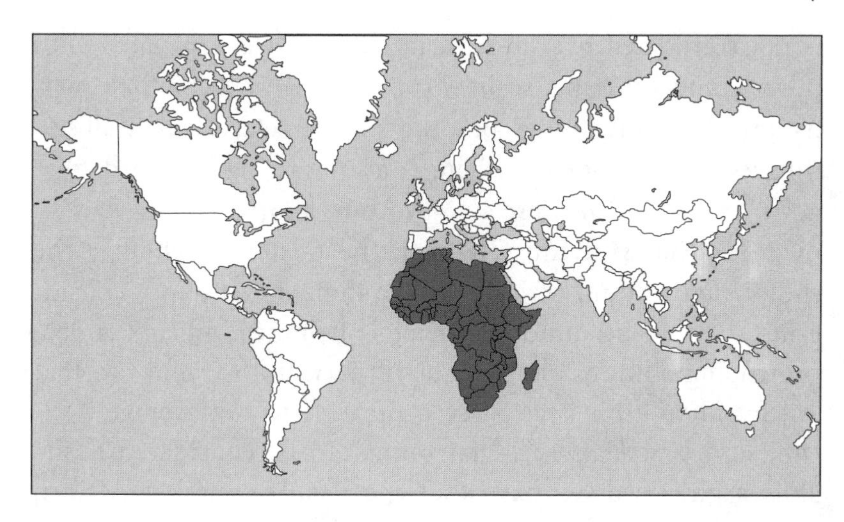

there are many references to these young women and their effect on their societies. Phrases such as: '*o bopegile*'—'she is well shaped'; '*seponono se likoti marameng*'—'a pretty girl who has dimples on her cheeks'; '*sematsatsa*'—'dazzling'; and '*semomonthane*'—'delectable'—illustrate the qualities possessed by some of these beauties who drove men to frenzy. They also brought much consternation to their families, on account of the attention that they drew to themselves.

Beauty in Indigenous Cultures

In traditional society, some of the features of a beautiful girl are: well-rounded hips; good firm breasts; round cheeks; dimples; full lips; and lovely clear skin that looks as if it's been 'licked by a snake' or 'washed with milk'. Unlike in the West, an African beauty is supposed to be well fed and healthy, with a buxom body and shapely legs. In traditional African culture it was unheard of for young girls to dabble with cigarettes, so there was never any problem with girls retaining their bright, clear eyes, good complexions and a set of strong, white teeth. If a girl was healthy, she would generally have lovely, shiny skin too. Even today, when 'thin' is so much the 'in thing', Africans are not crazy about skinny legs and bodies. Being skinny is not considered sexy in African culture. It is associated with poverty and suffering, so how can you then ascribe that quality to a beautiful thing? Basotho people refer disdainfully to thin legs as '*menotoane*'. There is also a saying in Sepedi that goes, '*Nku re reka mosela*'—'We buy a sheep by its tail'—meaning that you can tell from the posterior whether the sheep is fat or thin. Africans have a thing about bums, considering them to be quite a sensuous attribute. Large, rounded, protruding bottoms are particularly sexy. In the same way that '*menotoane*'—'thin legs'—are a turn-off to the average African, so are '*seshoapha*'—'flat bums'. To be considered desirable, a girl needs to have that specifically rounded 'African heritage' prominent in her anatomy. The natural African shape seems to incline towards a sexy posterior and most African women, even the skinny ones, are gifted in that way to some degree. There are a whole variety of traditional dances that play on this feature and involve a lot of flirting and teasing with the behinds. Nice big boobs, shaped like watermelons, are also considered a turn-on. Author Zakes Mda has a talent for describing beautiful African women in his novels in a way that is oh so sensuous!

Beauty Includes Good Character

But beauty, in African terms, is not only determined by physical attributes. In traditional society good character has always been considered integral to the notion of beauty. No matter how beautiful a girl might be in appearance, she was also expected to be a hard worker, as well as respectful of the elders and her culture. These qualities were considered as important as the component of physical beauty. '*Motho ea motle re mo bona ka diketso tsa hae*'—'You see a beautiful person through her deeds'. If you had beautiful features, chiseled cheekbones and a balanced bone structure but you were rude to people and rebelled at being given orders by adults, no one would think of you as remotely pretty.

Even though the missionaries and other white authorities regarded indigenous culture as uncivilised and did their best to undermine and discredit it, many African communities continued to live in the old traditional ways and practised their customs as they formerly had, albeit often in secrecy. In this regard, ironically, the government-proclaimed Bantustans and neglected rural areas played a crucial role in that they remained the custodians of local customs and culture and kept ethnic traditions intact.

In places such as the former Bantustans of Transkei and Zululand recognition was given to indigenous custom through retaining traditional laws. It was in the far-flung 'homelands' that Africans could truly be themselves and exercise their customs and culture without interference. Because these tribal areas were so remote and far removed from the urban melting pots, Western influence and authority was at a minimum there, and traditional culture remained largely uninterfered with. . . .

As a rule, South African black women are quite voluptuous and have no intention of being something else, so they say. They prefer to see the media depicting images they can relate to, rather than what is dictated or foreign to them.

Black Africans Are Tired of Western Images

From recent interviews and debates about beauty going on in the country it is apparent that black people are now tired of the Western images they have had to bear with over the centuries. They want to be their own masters and mistresses in determining how they perceive beauty and life in general. They want to be role players in decision-making and in the business sector, and influence industry policy to their benefit. And they want to be taken seriously as they contribute towards the economy of the country.

As a rule, South African black women are quite voluptuous and have no intention of being something else, so they say. They prefer to see the media depicting images they can relate to, rather than what is dictated or foreign to them. Affirmations such as 'beauty is from within', 'it is in the eye of the beholder', and 'there is no such thing as an ugly person' are being punted, rather than the emphasis on purely physical beauty. More and more magazines are showing ordinary people as models in their fashion pages alongside the idealised images of professionals.

As South Africa dabbles with this kind of 'political correctness', other societies have already tried and discarded it, finding that it hasn't quite caught on. Media has created such an escapist illusion that people still want to see a dream that they can strive towards, even if that means trying to look like someone else. Is it any wonder that cosmetic surgery is doing so well? If people were telling the truth about wanting to be accepted for who they are, they would not be spending so much money on those nips and tucks, boob enlargements, Botox lips and false hair.

An article by Heidi Kingstone in the *Saturday Star*, headed, 'Reality Is a Very Scary Beast', makes for entertaining reading. It is about a Dove ad campaign that Kingstone saw in the London underground in the month the campaign had just been launched. The advert [advertisement] displayed six girls in 'hideous white underwear' who were clearly not models, 'showing all their glorious imperfections' but supposedly entirely comfortable and happy with who they were. Kingstone obviously did not buy that and made her scepticism [skepticism] clear about the success of the campaign. She pointed out that Marks & Spencer had tried something similar in the 90s, which had failed. 'Magazine covers from time to time also try the same ploy but always revert to the tried and tested formula of using beautiful girls.'

Despite the hype to the contrary, looking beautiful still seems to be an essential part of a woman's life, even more so than before. Gone are the days when beauty parlours and products were the domain of beauty queens and models only. Young black girls are now dabbling with beauty aids much more than their mothers and aunts did.

Beauty Pageants Are Here to Stay

What about beauty pageants? Black, white, blue or green girls—is there still a need for an event based on the notion of physical beauty? Whichever way feminists view them, the pageants seem here to stay. Whatever debates there are about this concept of beauty seem mainly to be about *how*, and not whether the events should be done. Most women believe there *is* value in the contests. Young girls see them as a stepping-stone towards gaining recognition and financial muscle to facilitate whatever their ultimate goals might be. As the debates rage on, in some sectors the call is to have a complete overhaul of beauty pageants as they stand and change their image to an African one. What does that mean? Recently *City Press*, the biggest black weekend newspaper, had their third annual glamorous beauty pageant. The front page showed a picture of Miss City Press with the caption: 'And the Distinctly African Queen Is. . . .' The queen in question has short, boyishly cropped and styled hair and an athletic physique, looking more like a lovely Ndebele model than a beauty queen (Ndebele women tend to favour short, boyishly styled hair). Sello Chicco Twala, a musician and producer, thinks South Africa should be bold enough to transform Miss SA [South Africa] and make it African. 'The theme, dress code and everything about it should just be African,' he says. This does not necessarily mean that only black girls are intended to win.

Tembeka Nkamba-Van Wyk, who runs a beading company called 'Talking Beads' and is herself quite a big woman, also believes the contest should be one where African girls are free to express their natural heritage, in the sense of being well-endowed and not having false long hair. In her view, the judges will need to be scrutinised to ensure 'African sentiments'.

Beauty has had a direct impact on our lifestyle and health. The more we worry about the way we look and how the public perceives us, the more we spend to get that elusive 'right' look. Billions of rands [1 rand = about 14 cents US] are spent on diets that will give us the 'right' calories to have an acceptable figure. With the pressures of modern life, there have been more eating disorders than ever before. Psychologists are having a field day, what with having to counsel people who fall victim to peer pressure, either eating too much out of worry or not eating at all.

Then there are the visits to French clinics in quest of that perfect body, and to dermatologists for the ideal skin. Remember the Roaccutane cases a few years back with regard to acne? Roaccutane is a drug manufactured by Roche pharmaceuticals for patients with severe acne. A number of parents had complained that one of the side effects was terrible mood swings, which had caused their teenagers to become suicidal. There were lengthy debates going on among dermatologists, pharmacists, doctors and psychologists as to whether there was a causal link between Roaccutane and emotional disorders. The argument put forth by the Roche team was that many of those with severe acne are prone to depression because of their physical appearance, not because of the drug, and that Roaccutane, by improving scarring actually improves confidence and self-esteem. Whatever the outcome of the debate, it shows the lengths to which we will go to in order to have acceptable looks. It's obviously worse for teenagers, who are subject to a lot of peer pressure.

What about plastic surgery, which can be painful and not even have the desired results, and liposuction which, when not performed properly, can be fatal? In South Africa black women became scared of liposuction after the much-publicised case

African American Women Need to be Liberated from White Ideals

Much like the "Black is Beautiful" campaigns of the 1970s, African American women need to be liberated from the confines of white-dominated standards of beauty. A womanist black beauty liberation campaign would encompass a black or woman of color whose beauty issues (e.g., body image, hair, and race) are brought in from the margin to the center in an attempt to honor the beauty in her that has been reviled, rebuffed, and ignored. To be a black beauty liberationist means that you are not identified with the powers that be, but rather directly challenge the white supremacist hegemony that has kept your beauty and your body invisible, marginalized, and stereotyped.

Tracey Owens Patton,
"Hey Girl, Am I More than My Hair? African American Women and Their Struggles with Beauty, Body Image, and Hair,"
National Women's Studies Association Journal, *Summer 2006.*

of charming Soweto socialite, Pinky Moshoeshoe, who died after her surgery went horribly wrong in the 80s. Pinky had a lovely face and skin but was on the big side. One morning she booked herself into a private clinic in Hillbrow for liposuction so that she could come out looking slim and surprise her partner, family and friends. But she never came out.

Preoccupation with Looking Young

The South African society is currently too preoccupied with the 'young look'. Women, especially, suffer from the age syndrome because they are the ones most affected by the pressure not to age. As a result, they can be quite cagey about their age, since it affects job opportunities and their relationships. Many jobs are determined by age. That tower of fiefdom, Hollywood, that is always dictating to the world who the most beautiful or sexiest women are, isn't helping either. The leading women they cast are nearly always young, below 35 (and getting younger by the day)—and 98% white! What does that say to a young black girl growing up who has aspirations to make it in the beauty industry?

South African women should take their example from the French women, who seem to be ageless and become more confident as they grow older. It is not unusual to see French movies featuring women in their 50s and 60s playing sexy roles.

The decade of the 90s was a very good one for black girls in the beauty industry. From 1992 onwards, an estimated 70 per cent of Miss South Africas were black. 1999 saw the crowning of the first ever Miss Universe of African descent, Mpule Kwelagobe of Botswana. In 2000 Agbani Darego from Nigeria won Miss World. Since its launch in 1998 Face of Africa has produced a bevy of beautiful girls making it in international modelling. Cosmetic houses are at last beginning to see the value of using black faces for the branding of their products. More and more African girls are now taking modelling seriously, and there are also quite a few black photographers willing to venture into the sacred waters of fashion and beauty, formerly reserved for only the privileged few. Now if we can only have more black manufacturers, perhaps there will be more black faces doing the branding for those products.

Herman Mashaba is someone who believes in the value of beauty pageants. He feels they are a big stepping-stone for girls wanting to make it in the industry. Black Like Me held its first contest in 1987. The winner, Malepule Mabokela, who is now a medical doctor, was the brand for the product in that year. Mashaba feels it was a mistake not to follow through with those contests. 'If we don't run these campaigns ourselves we fall into a rut,' he says. 'If we can make sure that black girls are represented and get the recognition they deserve then our competitors will follow suit.'

Dr John Kani, asked in a private interview for his comment on beauty pageants, related this story: 'A few years ago I was having a discussion with some black American friends of mine and you know what they said?' His friends had apparently remarked that in America, when blacks were complaining that more white girls were winning beauty pageants than black girls, the organisers decided to bring in more black judges. It turned out that the black girls were actually doing much better when there were only white judges! 'Blacks seem to feel that they must always be neutral when given positions of power,' Kani said. 'Most times blacks are really their own worst enemies. When they are given opportunities, they should try to make the most of them for their own advantage.'

How long will black women be waiting for handouts to be dished to them by a society that has no intention of turning them into heroines? The black communities need to do that for themselves.

There Are No Absolute Ideals of Beauty

Nkwenkwe Nkomo sums it up this way: 'Beauty as a concept is a constant thing. As to what constitutes it there are variables. What constitutes a beautiful woman now has a range—there are no absolutes, e.g., from dark to light. Look at the Williams sisters [tennis players Serena and Venus], they are beautiful for what they stood for.' He regards the fascination with beauty as an innate force that has influenced the dynamics of attraction between a boy and girl, or man and woman from the time *Homo sapiens* carried a *kirrie* to protect his woman. 'That innate force has not changed, we have only cloaked it with civilization,' he says.

Is the industry intransigent to the needs of black women? Is it beginning to see beyond colour? Admittedly, there are quite a few girls who have broken barriers but is the pace fast enough? The challenges really are this: How long will black women be waiting for handouts to be dished to them by a society that has no intention of turning them into heroines? The black communities need to do that for themselves.

According to Carl Heunis of G3 Models, black models currently get the best-paid jobs. 'The big campaigns these days, it's always a black guy getting the lead,' he says. Time will tell if that is for real.

When Halle Berry, considered by many to be one of the most beautiful women in the world today, won the coveted Oscar for Best Actress for *Monster's Ball*, it was a triumph for black women. The 74th Academy Awards on 25 March 2002 was the first time ever that a black woman had won the Best Actress award. A very emotional Berry, with tears streaming down her face, dedicated her award to all the African American women who had struggled before her to make it in Hollywood. She said: 'This moment is so much bigger than me. It's for every nameless, faceless woman of colour that now has a chance because this door tonight has been opened.' When asked backstage if Hollywood was colour blind, Berry said: 'I hope this means they won't see our colour. That's what makes us so unique. I just hope we maybe will start to be judged on our work, and not our skin.'

In 2005 for the first time the Miss South Africa winner, Nokuthula Sithole, an engineering student at Wits [University of the Witwatersrand], as well as her two runners-up, Avumile Qongqo from Queenstown, and Matapa Maila from Pretoria, were all black. One of the contest judges, Carol Bouwer, producer of the magazine programme *Motswako* on SABC 2, said when interviewed in December 2005: 'We are at a point where we do not care about colour anymore'—meaning that the girls are now judged only on merit. She concluded: 'It gives me pride that any of the five black entrants could have walked away with the prize.'

VIEWPOINT 4

Black Women Use Hairstyles to Define Themselves

Regina Jere-Malanda

In the following viewpoint, Regina Jere-Malanda, editor of New African Woman, *considers the political aspects of black women's hairstyles. She describes how the natural look of the Afro of the 1960s implies a radical political stance, while the more recent straighter, smoother look as exemplified by America's First Lady, Michelle Obama, indicates a more mainstream political outlook.*

As you read, consider the following questions:

1. What message does Jere-Malanda think a *New Yorker* cartoon image of Michelle Obama with an Afro sends about the hairstyle?
2. What happened when Congresswoman Cynthia McKinney changed her hairstyle to cornrows?
3. What did editor Ashley Baker say about black hairstyles in a speech on hairstyles in the workplace? How did people react to what she said?

Black women today rarely wear their hair naturally. Next to skin colour, hair is truly the other most visible stereotype of being a black woman. Physically, socially, economically and stylistically, black women's hair is, indeed, not just hair. It is a big deal which evokes serious debate, and here is why:

Regina Jere-Malanda, "Black Women's Politically Correct Hair," *New African Woman*, December 2008, pp. 14–18.

In the late 1960s, the Afro or natural look became one of the emblems of Black Power, as popularised by the iconic [political activist] Angela Davis. It became a reflection of political and cultural progressiveness, as well as self-esteem, among black people. Fast forward to December 2008, the hairstyle that said "I'm black and proud", has almost disappeared, replaced by sleek fake-hair weaves and hair extensions or, worse still, hair straightened into submission through chemical creams.

Black Women's Hair Is a Serious Topic

For those of you who may feel a topic of black women's hair is just another frothy fashion issue, think again. Just try to follow some blogsphere debates in the run-up to the just-ended historic White House race to see just how Michelle Obama's hair took its own political trail.

Check out, for example, the controversial cartoon cover of the *New Yorker* magazine which depicted the Obamas in the Oval Office at the White House, in which Michelle is sporting an Afro and carrying [an] AK-47 [rifle]. Satire, it was claimed. But to many black people, the message was clear: Afro = angry and militant, reinforcing the age-old prejudice against natural black hair.

But there was even more in cyberspace, as many black women's blogs dedicated entire forums to debating Michelle's hair. For good reason, in some instances. One [blog] in particular—The Politics of Michelle Obama's Hair by Patricia J. Williams—was quite revealing. Although quoted rather at length here for emphasis, her views are, however, just scratching the surface of the hair issue, whose roots run deep, very deep.

Natural Hairstyles Are Considered Dangerous

"When I graduated from law school in the mid-1970s," says Williams, "African-American women's hair was constantly be-

African American Standards for Hair Date Back to Slavery

Historically, for many African Americans, "A lot of it has to do with [the] fact that the ability to be seen as American and not foreign or 'other' had a lot to do with their look," [African American studies professor Mark Anthony] Neal said. "Because skin color couldn't change, hair became a way to articulate a sense of American-ness. If kinkiness marked them as foreign, the ability to straighten hair marked them as more acceptable to the mainstream or 'American.'"

During slavery, African Americans of mixed white, black and Native American ancestry were seen as more valuable and more attractive because their lighter skin and straighter hair was closer in texture to whites.

Halimah Abdullah and William Douglas, "For Many Black Women, Hair Tells the Story of Their Roots," McClatchy Newspapers, October 9, 2009. www.mcclatchydc.com.

ing scrutinized for signs of subversion: the more 'natural' the more dangerous. So we pressed our hair flat with the weight of other people's expectations and waited for times to change. While curly hair, twists, short Afros, and cornrows are all much more prevalent and tolerated these days, those choices are still publicly interrogated to an unseemly degree. Lani Guinier, Bill Clinton's nominee to head the civil rights division of the Justice Department, was deemed radical in part because of what some commentators called her 'strange hair.' Similarly, when Cynthia McKinney [the congresswoman who stood as presidential candidate for the little-known Green

Party in the November elections. Yes, there were two black candidates in this election!] changed her hairstyle to cornrows, the [US] Capitol security guards blocked her way, claiming they didn't recognize her as a member of Congress."

"Most recently," she continues, "in the most discussed *New Yorker* magazine cover ever, what stood out for me was that Michelle Obama's putative politics were satirized via an Afro! Angela Davis hair! Yes, friends, the hairdo that crossword-puzzle enthusiasts find regularly described as a four-letter synonym for the fashion sensibility of protesters, armed revolutionaries, and frat boys yukking it up in 'fright wigs'. We're talking unequivocally, implacably, no bones about it, political hair. Regardless of how differently the real Davis may wear her hair today, her coif is remembered as a mathematically precise series of explosions, of radioactive microwaves pulsing outward from the sun of the universalised angry black scalp".

Yes, black women globally couldn't help but notice and discuss Michelle's perfectly coiffed tresses—and in as much as we were moved and inspired by her devotion-filled speeches in support of her husband and country's future—we also wanted to know: Who does her hair? What hair products does she use? Is her hair chemically straightened? And so forth.

Gladly, *New African Woman* has reliably learnt that Michelle Obama is a no-lye lady! That is, she does not chemically straighten her hair—if true, this is good news to millions of black womenfolk still in search of that chemical-free hair nirvana. In fact, the First Lady-in-waiting's mane is the handiwork of a hither to little-known California-based stylist, Johnny Wright of Frederic Fekkai, the famous creator of celebrity hairstyles and hair-care products, who is also a consultant for the big black-hair brand SoftSheen-Carson. Wright is also reported to be the magic hands behind the hairstyles of celebrities Vanessa Williams, Anita Baker and Vivica A. Fox.

Hairstyles Influence How Global Society Perceives Black Women

Indeed, while every society in the world has come up with ways, gadgets and products to groom itself for beauty purposes, black women's hair goes far beyond mere sprucing up and aesthetics. With its history of deep roots in slavery and its politics that change many people's viewpoints, it's a marker of femininity that can influence how the global society embraces the black woman in both political and social circles. How else can society explain this outrageous scenario at a New York law firm which invited Ashley Baker, then associate editor of the prominent glossy beauty magazine *Glamour*, to speak to them on the "Dos and Don'ts of Corporate Fashion". In a slide show, she says about a black woman in an Afro hairdo: "A real no-no! As for dreadlocks, how truly dreadful! Shocking that some people still think it's appropriate to wear those hairstyles at the office. No offence, but those political hairstyles really have to go."

Although she resigned soon after, following public outrage and *Glamour* issuing a grovelling apology, Baker touched many raw nerves among black women, including Afro-wearing Dr Venus Opal Reese, who said in reaction: "When it comes to race, we're looking from the past. When people see me with my natural hair, they don't see Dr Venus Opal Reese who has four degrees, they see an historical idea of what natural hair means. And that's what it meant in the 1970s and 1960s; it equalled Black Nationalism and was linked to the Black Panther Party. It was considered militant. That doesn't mean it's true now, but that's how it's linked." Dr Reese, who is assistant professor of Aesthetics and Cultural Studies at the University of Texas in Dallas, connects hair with culture and politics, whether as an attempt to conform or as a way to declare a revolution. "Some people know wine. I pay attention to hair. I've spent a long time looking at identity formation through hair."

Sad but true, these days the natural Afro look is widely considered unattractive by many black women (and men), and, as such, not considered fashionable. The past 30 years have seen the Afro replaced by the likes of Jheri curl and dreadlocks in the '80s, braiding, cornrows, locks, and twists in the '90s, and today's rave, the straight-as-a-ruler look—chemically processed black hair that mimics Caucasian or Asian hair texture and styles—as well as the increasingly popular hair extensions, sown on or glued, to hide the natural look, or the sleek-looking wigs, favoured by women like rapper P Diddy's mother, who is famed for her blonde wigs. To proponents of the natural look, however, chemically straightening Afro hair, or hiding it under fake extensions, is a sign of embracing white superiority over being black, and hence indicates self-hate.

With its history of deep roots in slavery and its politics that change many people's viewpoints, [black hair is] a marker of femininity that can influence how the global society embraces the black woman in both political and social circles.

Hairstyles Mark Major Life Events in Africa

But there is even more to black women's hair in the context of continental Africa. In different countries and communities, hairstyles mean different things. For example, a symbol of woman's marital status, a religious ritual, a mark of ethnicity and geographical origins or even age. In many southern African countries, when a young girl comes of age, her hair is shaven off to symbolise that milestone, and the same ritual is practiced in other areas, when a woman has just been widowed.

As David [B.] Coplan, a professor in anthropology at South Africa's Wits University [University of the Witwatersrand], reckons in *True Love* magazine: "We judge people by appearances and, to an extent, hairstyles signify something about you, so it's natural for people to make assumptions about you based on the way you've styled your hair. Hair and identity are inseparable—whether you're consciously making a statement or not, your hairstyle does express something about you. So if you've been thinking your hair is making no declaration to the world, think again."

Yolanda Chapman, who has done extensive research on global attitudes towards black women's hairstyling practices, believes that black women have struggled to define themselves in positive terms as both black and female. "Dealing with issues of beauty—particularly skin colour, facial features, and hair texture—is one concrete example of how controlling images denigrate black women. Hair, then, is a key site for investigating how black women's identities are circumscribed by dominant discourses on race and gender. Since black women have had to learn how to adapt to their sexist and racist environments, one survival strategy they created was 'shifting.'" She explains shifting as a change of outward behaviour, to adopt an alternate pose or voice or embellish a certain identity, in order to satisfy others such as white people or black men.

She also explains how in the "Black is Beautiful" movement in the 1960s, hair became such a key determinant in visually declaring black pride through embracing natural styles, such as the Afro and various braiding styles. After two centuries of slavery, writes Chapman, a self-created system of black hair care was created in the late 1800s with the birth of the black hair-care boom, followed in the early 1900s, by Madam C.J. Walker and Annie Malone, who are famed for creating the massive empire of hair-grooming products targeted at African American women. Malone wanted, for example, to solve hair problems, such as baldness and breakage, that many black women of the time faced as a result of a high-stress lifestyle, a nutritionally deficient diet, and inadequate hygiene. But how things have changed.

VIEWPOINT 5

Brazilian Women Are Confident About Their Beauty

Judy Bachrach

Editor and journalist Judy Bachrach interviewed a number of prominent Brazilians about the popular belief that Brazilian women are more beautiful than women from other countries. In the following viewpoint, Bachrach considers topics such as the genetic ancestry of Brazilians, plastic surgery, tanning, and waxing—all of which contribute to their beauty. She also details how Brazilian women define beauty.

As you read, consider the following questions:

1. What qualities does model Geane Brito say make a Brazilian beauty?
2. What percentage of Brazilian women would consider cosmetic surgery? How do they compare to women from other countries?
3. According to Brito, why is waxing important to Brazilian women?

Of all the injustices women must put up with, one of the worst is that the majority of us are not born Brazilian. This is quite a dilemma—and not because everyone there is a ringer for Gisele [Bündchen], a beauty around whom a certain degree of controversy swirls (amazing, but the local think-

Judy Bachrach, "The Girls from Ipanema," *Allure*, July 1, 2006, p. 148.

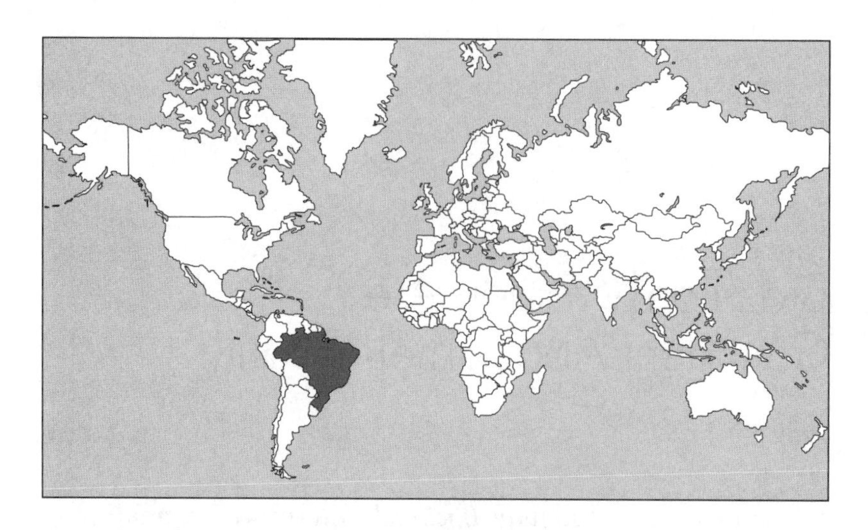

ing is she's too Nordic and too slender). Besides, a number of Brazilian women, blonde or otherwise, consider themselves supermodel-gorgeous, according to a recent study by a Harvard Medical School psychologist.

That's right. More Brazilians believe themselves beautiful than the female inhabitants of ten other nations examined. That's more than twice the number of aesthetically secure U.S. women and far more than women of Japan, where exactly zero percent claimed to like their own looks (on the other hand, they may have just been aiming for modesty, which is not a famous Brazilian trait).

But why shouldn't Brazilians acknowledge the obvious? Being Brazilian is basically a form of visual incitement, a passport to idolatry: The girl from Ipanema flashes on the screen, and men wish themselves south of the equator. Meanwhile, other women are left in the dust—especially the ones with large breasts (considered excessive in Brazil) and butts as flat as Iowa farmland. Brazil, according to her female citizens, is butt heaven. "Brazilian women all want to have a big butt," the model Caroline Ribeiro explains from São Paolo, sighing heavily. "And I don't have a big butt, so it was very hard growing up. I felt very bad."

Yes, even Brazilians have difficulty being Brazilian: The aesthetic stakes are so high, the standards at once elastic and yet difficult to attain. You can be blonde or brunette ("Really, I think the Brazilian man wants both types in his bed," says a resigned beauty who has sworn off the attentions of her countrymen), but whatever you are, you have to be gorgeous. And the first and most important step is to: Buy into the Brazilian beauty myth.

More Brazilians believe themselves beautiful than the female inhabitants of ten other nations examined.

Characteristic of Brazilian Beauty

The honey-throated actress Sônia Braga (late of *Sex and the City* and the star of the acclaimed movie *Dona Flor and Her Two Husbands*) reports that for the longest time, she thought true sensuality was embodied by Marilyn Monroe and refinement by Grace Kelly. As for herself: "I played only characters who were neurotic and shy, because that's what I was. A shy girl from São Paolo. I had no connection with the ocean, no idea about the sexuality in the characters. Never in my life did it cross my mind that there was some kind of beauty out there for me!"

Then, at the age of 24, Braga landed the role of "the most gorgeous character ever written," as she describes it, in the cast of a Brazilian TV drama called *Gabriela, Cravo e Canela.*

"Gabriela, Clove and Cinnamon," Braga translates, "because the character's skin was the color of cinnamon and she smelled like cloves, and she was the best cook on the planet. And in bed, too, the best!" Almost instantly, Braga explains, "I became a sex symbol." She was imbued with the idea of "how beautiful Brazilian women are. Before that, I thought about us Brazilians as ordinary human beings like anybody else."

This, clearly, was a mistake.

Brazilian notions of beauty are based on firm aesthetic guidelines, some unique to the country. Worse luck for outsiders: A number of these attributes are the result of pure genetic good fortune.

"To be a Brazilian beauty you need more curves; you are at least a size 8," explains Geane Brito, a Brazilian-born former Calvin Klein model, who has the misfortune of being a size 4. "When they say, 'Ahhhh, you're Brazilian! You're fantastic!'—in order to fulfill that image, you have to have long glossy hair, a good body, and a dazzling smile. But the most important is . . . here it comes again . . . the ass. A good ass."

Beautiful Ancestors Contribute to Brazilians' Beauty

"Like me," model Fernanda Tavares explains. "I have black ancestors, Portuguese, everything. My grandfather's grandfather came to Brazil, and he married an Indian woman, and my grandmother's grandmother was a slave. I love that I have this mix."

"I am a typical Brazil beauty," says Brito, who, like most of her countrywomen, has no use for false humility. "I am Indian, black, and white, with big lips, brown eyes, and long black hair. When I first started modeling in the '80s, Brazil didn't want that kind of beauty. Parisians found me gorgeous, though. Now we're considered beautiful in Brazil. What we are is warm from the beach. When I asked an ex-boyfriend, "Why do you love girls from Rio so much?" He said, 'Because their bodies are always warm.' I'll never forget that."

And yet, she adds (and this is the inherent contradiction), all this female warmth has its drawbacks: an excessive willingness to please; a tendency to view beauty as a moral triumph and, at the same time, a kind of dowry to be laid at the feet of men. "Definitely the Brazilian woman is very repressed, by and large," Brito says with a small sigh. "From the outside you see the poetry of her, the beautiful smile. A warm woman with hair, kindness, and a beautiful body. But behind all that beauty," Brito notes, "there is suffering."

Darker, Thicker Skin Helps Brazilians Tan

"Sunbathing is like a cult down here and has been for many, many years," says famed Brazilian plastic surgeon Luiz Toledo. "But in Brazil, a lot of women have thick skin and a bit darker skin, so there's more protection against the sun's rays."

However, this form of genetic good luck is by no means universally distributed. "Most women in southern Brazil are fair-skinned, and they do suffer the damaging effects of the sun," reports Doris Hexsel, a renowned dermatologist who practices in Rio and Porto Alegre. "I mean, they get photoaging and skin cancer, which is quite frequent around here."

Model Fernanda Tavares explains: "I have black ancestors, Portuguese, everything. My grandfather's grandfather came to Brazil, and he married an Indian woman, and my grandmother's grandmother was a slave. I love that I have this mix."

Many Brazilians Have Plastic Surgery

Ivo Pitanguy is generally considered to be the top plastic surgeon in Brazil, perhaps the best in the world, so when he speaks, it is with considerable authority. "One of the most beautiful things about a human being is the way she looks at herself," Pitanguy says from his São Paolo office. "And Brazilians, they look at themselves in a beautiful way, trying not to be neurotic and stressed. They are just a happy mixture of the races."

But if everyone is so happy and gorgeous, I wonder, why do Brazilian women demand so much plastic surgery? "Because Brazilians in general love an operating table," replies Brito. "And if you doubt this, all you have to do is look at the number of C-sections pregnant women have. Exactly. Brazilian women have a lot of confidence in Brazilian medicine. Look at Pitanguy—he's a household name."

Toledo observes that there is a significant reason for all this reliance on medical enhancements: "Plastic surgery flourishes in Brazil because we have very good surgeons with good training, who are not too worried about having their careers ended by lawsuits." And then what follows is the classic Brazilian equation: Great beauty equals achievement. "We have taught people in the media that they too could become a better person," says the plastic surgeon. "That they could have a better body, if they wanted to."

"Brazilian women are very self-critical; I think it has to do with our culture and its celebration of the perfect body and the perfect face."

Thus, more than 54 percent of Brazilian women claim they would consider cosmetic surgery, and 7 percent (more than twice the global average) admit having had it, according to Harvard Medical School psychologist Nancy Etcoff, who coheaded the study. "That's the highest of any country we examined," Etcoff says.

"Why?" echoes Toledo. "Because plastic surgery is not a matter of vanity, but of self-preservation. It's true. On your job, the next woman hired may be employed because she looks younger than you, more prepared and active."

But there's more than pragmatism involved in this search for perfection. There are societal expectations. "Brazilian women are very self-critical; I think it has to do with our culture and its celebration of the perfect body and the perfect face," says dermatologist Hexsel. "Sometimes I have patients who say, 'I have my first wrinkle. Please take it away!' I tell them, 'You're so pretty; please wait.' But they don't believe it!"

Actually, they do believe it. They just want to be even better.

"I always knew I'd be a model, and I was very vain even when I was little—I think even more than I am now, if that's possible," recalls Tavares. She was exactly three when she began picking out her own clothes; ten when her vigilant mother ("who wouldn't let me run down the street because I might fall or scratch my legs, and models can't have scratches") enrolled her in a modeling course. "And I loved the modeling course!" says Tavares. At 14, she moved to São Paolo and began her career in earnest.

Tavares was different. "Love your butt! You're not skinny like those other women!" Stella McCartney once told her. "Don't lose weight!" (Tavares didn't: At five eleven, she's 128 pounds.)

But the best thing about being Brazilian is that you can save a fortune on cosmetics. "Makeup is not big in Brazil, because women love showing their real faces," Braga says. "We prefer tanning instead of makeup," Ribeiro says, echoing Braga. "And if we do wear makeup, it must feel natural. I love Terracotta blush by Guerlain."

Brazilians Spend Money on Waxing

"The biggest business in Brazil is waxing," reports Brito. "These bikini-waxing places are just huge, filled with women. You go in, take off [your] clothes, and boom—oh, my God, everyone can see your vagina! Personally, I like my privacy. But in Brazil? No! No privacy.

"Of course, there's a reason for all this waxing," she continues, by which she means tiny string bikinis. These are as essential to Brazilian beauties as couture is to the French, and they require the same careful grooming. "Yes, even with a big ass. That's one thing I find cool about the Brazilian woman. She's very comfortable with her body. She'll wear that bikini—even if she has cellulite."

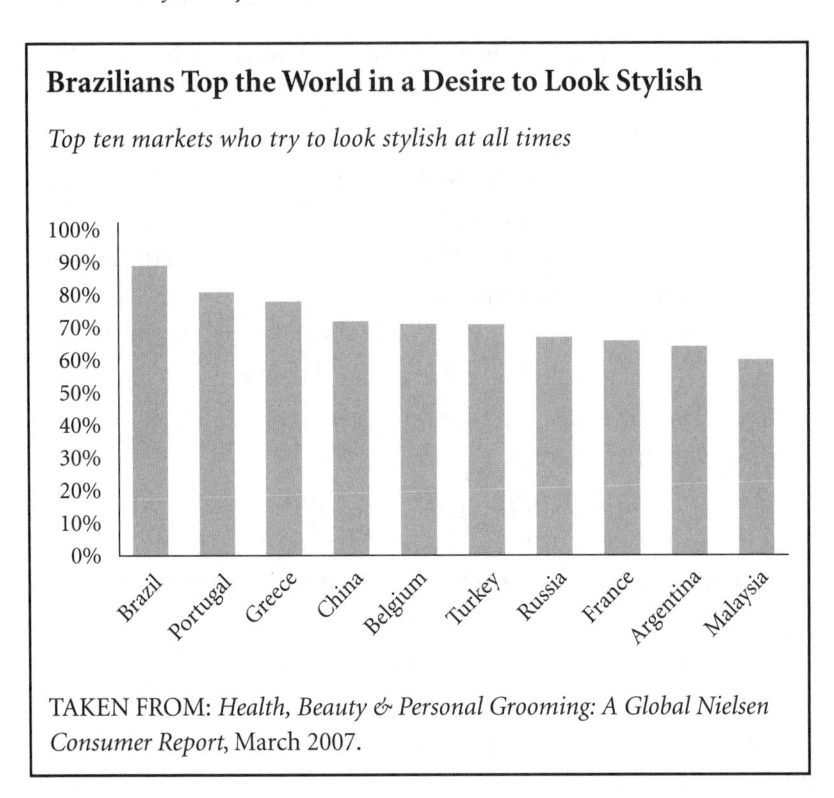

Brazilians Top the World in a Desire to Look Stylish

Top ten markets who try to look stylish at all times

TAKEN FROM: *Health, Beauty & Personal Grooming: A Global Nielsen Consumer Report*, March 2007.

She muses a bit. "This is still a very macho country. Until a few years ago, a jealous husband could shoot his wife if she was having an affair! Perhaps sex is the most powerful tool a Brazilian woman has. That's why she concentrates so much on her beauty."

Brazilians Believe Intelligence Is an Important Part of Beauty

"In Brazil, 92 percent of women believe intelligence is essential for beauty," reports Etcoff. "That's the highest percentage of any nation we studied, next to Italy. However, in Brazil everything is considered essential to beauty."

The psychologist rattles off what she means by "everything." Apparently 96 percent of Brazilian women also believe happiness is necessary for beauty, whereas good hair is only vital to 68 percent of the general female population. Brazilian women—71 percent of them—also think that financial success is vital to beauty. So is spiritual fulfillment: 72 percent.

Excuse me, I interrupt the psychologist: Spiritual fulfillment is necessary for beauty in Brazil?

In Brazil, 92 percent of women believe intelligence is essential for beauty.

"Yes," Etcoff says. "And so is sexiness: 82 percent of Brazilians think that to be sexy is a necessary component of beauty. Whereas in the United States, only 39 percent believe this."

Boy, are we seriously puritanical, I say.

"That's right," agrees Etcoff. "Brazilians are, in many ways, confident about themselves, although they did tell us beauty was, in part, mandated by their society and was essential for success. But they also want to see beauty as a whole, as part of their personality."

And as she speaks, I am reminded of my conversation with Sônia Braga. "I love beauty, I do, in men and women. There's a poster here of that show you have in the States—*Nip/Tuck*—I see it in L.A. Thank God I am not driving, because there's such a beautiful body on that poster. When I see Gisele Bündchen, for instance, I cannot stop staring at her. Well, because she is so beautiful. So gorgeous. What can I do about it? I simply cannot stop!"

A brief pause, as she considers her own career, where she has assumed the personae of any number of beauties. Braga ticks them off with considerable pride: "Prostitute, bitch, heroine! And they all dress in different ways. You can choose which one you want to be."

As long as she's Brazilian.

Periodical Bibliography

The following articles have been selected to supplement the diverse views presented in this chapter.

Christal Brown et al.	"In the Eyes of the Beholder: Dancers and Choreographers Talk About What They Find Beautiful," *Dance Magazine*, July 2008.
Alene Dawson	"Hair in the Black Community: Roots of a Debate," *Los Angeles Times*, October 11, 2009.
Johannes Hönekopp	"Once More: Is Beauty in the Eye of the Beholder? Relative Contributions of Private and Shared Taste to Judgments of Facial Attractiveness," *Journal of Experimental Psychology: Human Perception and Performance*, April 2006.
Tina Ezell Hull	"More Black Women Embracing Their Hair's Natural Style," *Charlotte Observer* (Charlotte, NC), January 17, 2008.
Attillo Jesús	"That Global Look: China's New Faces," *Le Monde Diplomatique*, June 2005.
Sheena Magenya	"The Tyranny of Beauty: A Critical Look at Beauty and What It Means to Women Today," *Sister Namibia*, December 1, 2008.
Clare Murphy	"In the Eye of the Beholder?" BBC News Online, December 4, 2003. http://news.bbc.co.uk.
Tracey Owens Patton	"Hey Girl, Am I More than My Hair? African American Women and Their Struggles with Beauty, Body Image, and Hair," *National Women's Studies Association Journal*, Summer 2006.
Shilpa Raina	"Unfair Game: The Indian Obsession with Skin Colour," Thaindian News, August 30, 2009. www.thaindian.com.

CHAPTER 2

Body Image

VIEWPOINT 1

British Women Are Less Happy with Their Own Bodies than British Men

Barbara Lewis

A 2007 British survey queried twenty-five thousand young people between the ages of seventeen and thirty-five to find out how they felt about their bodies. In this viewpoint, reporter Barbara Lewis discusses the survey's findings and considers some of the social influences on people's perceptions of body image.

As you read, consider the following questions:

1. What did the survey report about how British young women felt about their bodies?
2. What did the survey say about men's attitudes about their bodies?
3. According to the author, how has modern media affected how women and men perceive their bodies?

Britain's young women have never appeared so confident. Many are outperforming men, grabbing the best jobs and planning to balance their fulfilling careers with motherhood. But they are also more obsessed than ever with physical appearance and would go to painful lengths to change it. BBC Radio commissioned the latest of many surveys into how

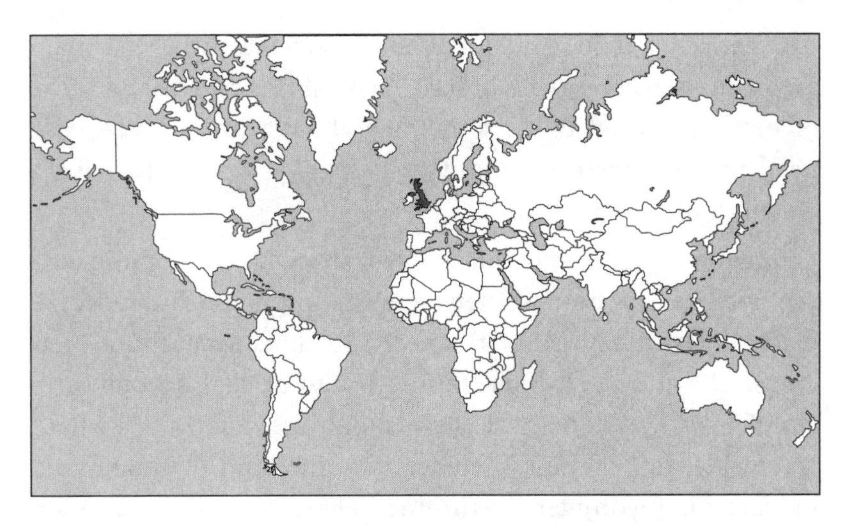

young Britons feel about their bodies—and found that far more women than men are unhappy about the way they look.

More than 50 per cent of the women questioned—compared with less than 25 per cent of men—said they would consider plastic surgery, according to a survey of around 25,000 people aged between 17 and 35 carried out by BBC Radio 1's Newsbeat programme and 1xtra TXU, a music programme aimed at young people.

Other findings included that 31 per cent of size 12 women described their bodies as overweight or fat, while 50 per cent of the women surveyed said there were many things they would change about their bodies; more than one in 10 said they hated their bodies.

By contrast, 49 per cent of men said they were "okay" with their appearance and one in 10 were "very happy" with it—according to the survey carried out between January 26 and February 9 this year [2007].

Terri Apter, a senior tutor at Newnham College, Cambridge, with expertise in development of young adults within society and the changing balance of work and family in women's lives, said she was not surprised by the survey's results. "It's consistent with other research," she said, especially that carried out in affluent, Western societies, where women are prime targets for big brands. "The aim is to create a sense of need. You need to do something about your wrinkles, you need to do something about your hair, you need to have a certain look," Apter said.

Men are targets too, but women, she said, were "more susceptible." "At the time women were gaining power in the workplace, there was no similar concern for liberation about their looks," she added. "I don't think it has to be that no one cares about how they look, but there should be a range of what's acceptable, rather than reference to some kind of model and in particular younger or thinner. There should be a much closer link between what functions well and what's attractive."

Britain's young women have never appeared so confident. Many are outperforming men, grabbing the best jobs and planning to balance their fulfilling careers with motherhood. But they are also more obsessed than ever with physical appearance and would go to painful lengths to change it.

The problem has gotten worse, as the sophistication of modern media, which constantly expose us to impossibly thin, computer-adjusted images, creates ever more elusive physical targets, especially for women. For men, the ideal of a strong physique portrayed by male models on the catwalk and in the media is relatively achievable.

Attempts to promote more natural-sized women models have had mixed success. Madrid fashion shows banned "size zero" (British size four) models with too low a body mass index—a measure based on weight and height—but London did not follow suit for this year's fashion week in February.

Some advertisers have also sought to present more realistic women. For instance, the Unilever brand of skin and hair-care

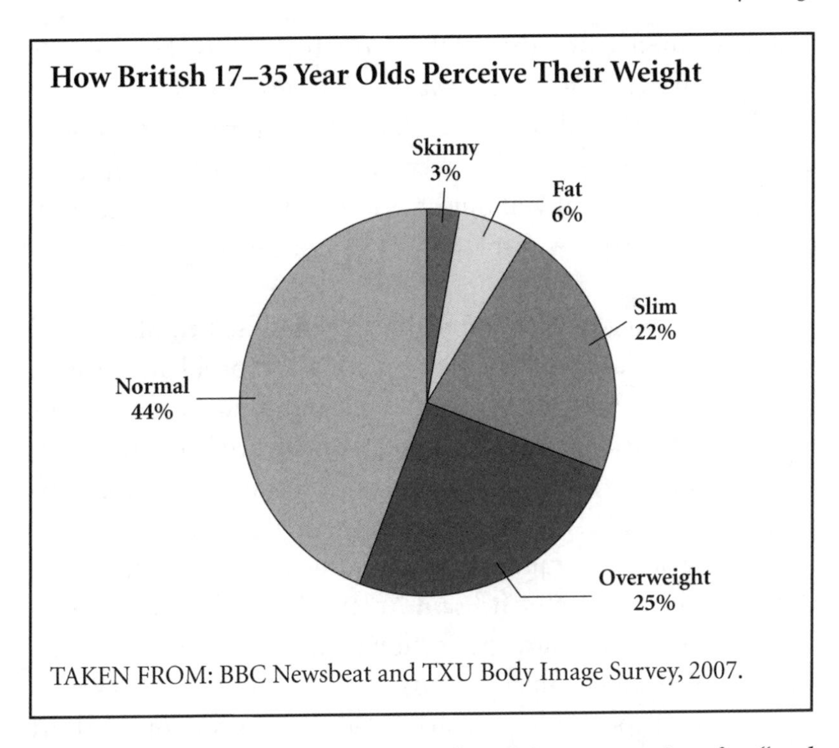

TAKEN FROM: BBC Newsbeat and TXU Body Image Survey, 2007.

products, Dove, has created an advertising campaign for "real beauty", using women with real rather than ideal body shapes. "The existing narrow definition of beauty is not only unrealistic and unattainable, but clearly it also creates hang-ups that can lead girls to question their own beauty," said Philippe Harousseau, US marketing director for Dove, in a press statement. "It's time to free the next generation from these stereotypes and give girls the tools they need to discover their own definition of beauty."

But, for every advertisement using a woman with a voluptuous figure, there are many more that use the perfectly thin to sell products. "How do you get around capitalist enterprise?" asked US academic Joan Jacobs Brumberg, professor of history, human development and gender studies at Cornell University. "It's very hard."

Providing historical evidence that the problem has evolved, Brumberg analysed more than 100 diaries written by girls and young women from the 1820s until the 1990s. Her results form the basis of a book, *The Body Project*, which has sold widely in the United States. "In the 19th century, most adolescent girls and young adults were very concerned about good works . . . it was really about character," she said. "In the 20th century, they were more and more concerned about good looks."

Apart from the media and big businesses, Brumberg said women were also guilty of perpetuating the problem through their obsession with their own bodies and drawing implicit or explicit comparisons with others. "Women need to stop reading each others' bodies," she said. "We have internalised appearance as the best indicator of how we are doing."

The most powerful antidote could be humour. "I think individuals try to counter it," said Apter, of the obsession with a narrow ideal of physical perfection. "Stand-up comics can do it." One of Britain's most famous female stand-up comics is Jo Brand, who shot to fame, wearing Doc Martens boots, a short haircut and clothes that made no apology for her definitely-not-size-zero figure.

Aware that female personalities were judged on their appearance, she told BBC Radio 4, "I tried to look as neutral as possible," although she admits that could have been interpreted as scruffiness. In any case, her reaction, once again, was very much a minority phenomenon.

VIEWPOINT 2

African Americans Hold Unique Opinions of the Ideal Body Image

Eric J. Bailey

In the following viewpoint, taken from his book Black America, Body Beautiful: How the African American Image Is Changing Fashion, Fitness, and Other Industries, *anthropologist Eric J. Bailey considers the body image of African Americans. He cites research studies of various age groups, from elementary school children to adults. He concludes that African Americans have an ideal body image that is larger than that of other Americans and that it is important for African Americans to retain their positive self-image rather than adopt European American ideals.*

As you read, consider the following questions:

1. What does Bailey mean by "flexible cultural definition of healthiness"?
2. What did the eighth- and ninth-grade African American girls studied say boys looked for in the "ideal girl"?
3. What does the author conclude is essential for African Americans to do?

Eric J. Bailey, *Black America, Body Beautiful: How the African American Image Is Changing Fashion, Fitness, and Other Industries*, Santa Barbara, CA: Praeger, 2008, pp. 24–33.

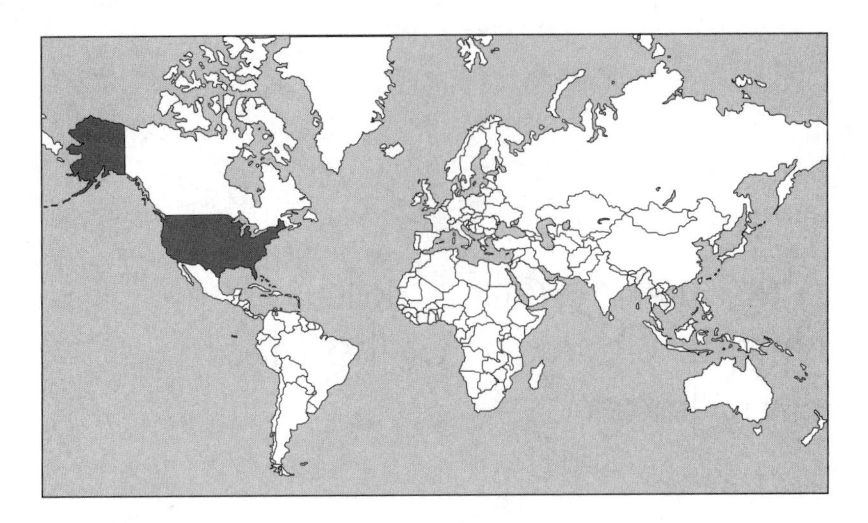

Think about how often you have heard or used the following phrases:

> That boy needs some meat on his bones!
>
> There's nothing wrong with him; he's just very "healthy."
>
> I like my women "thick," with some hips on them.
>
> Why are you exercising; you're going to be too thin!
>
> There's just more of me to love.
>
> There must be somethin' wrong with him/her—he/she looks like he/she lost some weight!

These comments, and so many more, reflect the African American perspective that for one to be healthy, he or she must be at least well proportioned (with noticeable hips, stomach, thighs, and breasts)—even bordering on overweight—and must definitely not be too thin (perceived as an indication of having contracted HIV/AIDS or of having an eating disorder). Moreover, these comments reflect the African American "flexible cultural definition of healthiness." This definition means, in other words, that it is good in the African American community to have some "meat on your bones," primarily because having such a body type indicates that one has more than enough food to eat and enough income and leisure time in which to consume the ample food.

On one hand, the "flexible cultural definition of healthiness" can actually be to the advantage of African Americans because it allows for varying degrees of acceptable body types within the culture, preventing a narrow definition of which body type constitutes the healthy one. On the other hand, the flexibility promotes acceptance of overweight and obesity as the norm within the African American community. As the more accepted and more ideal body type in the African American population becomes the heavier one, as opposed to the thinner one, tremendous medical and quality-of-life concerns (e.g., hypertension, diabetes, and cardiovascular disease) arise.

It is good in the African American community to have some "meat on your bones," primarily because having such a body type indicates that one has more than enough food to eat and enough income and leisure time in which to consume the ample food.

Nonetheless, the African American flexible cultural definition of healthiness is one that mainstream society actually wishes that it could truly embrace and incorporate into its culture and values pattern, for the preference for thinness within mainstream U.S. society has contributed to eating disorders such as anorexia and bulimia among white males and females. In addition to bearing the imprint of the cultural pattern of thinness, U.S. mainstream society receives constant messages and pressure through the media and at the workplace, and from the entertainment, fitness, and fashion industries to stay or to become thin.

To provide a better understanding of African American body image, size, and body type preferences, this [viewpoint] highlights several recent studies that examine the subject in the African American and other U.S. populations. This section is divided into four age- and school-based groupings: (1) elementary school, (2) middle and high school, (3) college, and (4) professional adults. The grouping of African Americans into age- and school-based categories will provide a better understanding of the variation and diversity of opinions within the African American population with regard to body image, body size, and body-type preferences.

Body Image in Elementary School

A study conducted in thirteen northern California public elementary schools, titled "Overweight Concerns and Body Dissatisfaction Among Third-Grade Children: The Impacts of Ethnicity and Socioeconomic Status," examined the prevalence of body image concerns and body dissatisfaction among third-grade girls and boys, as influenced by ethnicity, and socioeconomic status (SES). This study assessed overweight concerns; body dissatisfaction; and desired shape, height, and weight among 969 children (mean age, 8.5 years).

Of the 999 third-grade children enrolled in the thirteen schools, 969 (97.0 percent) participated in the study. Parents refused participation for 29 children, and 1 child was absent during the study. By ethnic breakdown, participants in the study were 44 percent white, 21 percent Latino, 19 percent Asian American (not including Filipino), 8 percent Filipino, 5 percent African American, 1 percent American Indian, and 1 percent Pacific Islander. Slightly more than 50 percent of the participants (50.2 percent) were girls, and boys in the sample were slightly older (8.5 years vs. 8.4 years) than girls. The researchers drew their data from responses to the Kids' Eating Disorders Survey (KEDS).

As hypothesized, the research team found that girls reported greater concern about overweight and greater body dissatisfaction, and desired thinner body shapes than boys. After accounting for sex differences, ethnic differences were assessed separately for boys and girls. Among girls, African Americans had significantly more overweight concerns than Asian Americans and Filipinos; and Latinas had significantly more overweight concerns than whites, Asian Americans, and Filipinos. White and Latina girls reported greater body dissatisfaction than Asian American girls.

To examine whether ethnic differences could be explained by differences in actual body fatness, comparisons were repeated after stratifying the girls into three body mass index (BMI) groups: (1) girls with a BMI *at or below* the 25th percentile for the entire sample; (2) girls with a BMI between the 25th and 75th percentile; and (3) girls with a BMI at or above the 75th percentile. Data indicated that overweight concerns and body dissatisfaction increased with increasing BMI in all ethnic groups.

After groups were stratified by BMI, significant ethnic differences in overweight concerns persisted only in the large middle stratum. Among these girls, Latinas reported significantly more overweight concerns than whites and Asian Americans, and there was a trend toward greater overweight concerns among African Americans compared with whites. There were no significant differences in body dissatisfaction or desired body shape among girls or among boys.

Overall, this study indicates that African American and Hispanic girls are not immune to cultural emphasis on extreme thinness. Latina and African American third-grade girls reported greater or equivalent levels of dysfunctional eating attitudes and behaviors in comparison with white girls, even after controlling for actual body fatness and SES. The findings suggest that body dissatisfaction and body image concerns are prevalent across sex, ethnicity, and socioeconomic class. They also indicate a need for culturally appropriate school-based primary prevention programs designed specifically for Latino and African American children.

In their study "Ideal Body Size Beliefs and Weight Concerns of Fourth-Grade Children," [Sharon H.] Thompson, [Sara J.] Corwin, and [Roger G.] Sargent explored whether preferences for body image, size, and type are formulated earlier than the junior high or high school years. This study assessed racial and gender differences in perceptions of ideal body size among white and African American fourth-grade children.

The researchers surveyed a random sample of fourth graders at small, medium, and large South Carolina elementary schools. The final sample of participants consisted of 817 fourth graders aged eight to twelve years (mean age = 9.3 years). Demographically, the sample comprised 51.8 percent white children and 48.2 percent African American children, of whom 51.4 percent were girls and 48.6 percent were boys. The survey collected information in the following areas: demographics, dieting and weight concern, body image, and body size perception.

When students were asked to select a picture that "looks most like you," the researchers found that among these fourth graders, African American males selected a larger self than white males. Additionally, African American females selected a significantly heavier self than white females. As for selecting an ideal female and male child size, African American females selected a larger female child than did white females.

Overall, this study indicates that even at this point in the sociocultural development of children, the factors of gender, SES, and ethnicity are of great influence in selecting ideal body size and in determining body size satisfaction. African American children selected significantly heavier ideal sizes than did white children for self, male child, adult male, and adult female.

Similarly, in their study titled "Discrepancies in Body Image Perception Among Fourth-Grade Public School Children from Urban, Suburban, and Rural Maryland," [Claudette]

Welch et al. found that African American elementary children chose larger figures than did whites and children of other races to represent their current and ideal images, and the African American children were most satisfied with their body size. The objective of this study was to determine whether there is an association between body image perception and weight status as measured by the BMI among a group of fourth graders in Maryland.

When students were asked to select a picture that "looks most like you," the researchers found that among these fourth graders, African American males selected a larger self than white males. Additionally, African American females selected a significantly heavier self than white females.

The sample consisted of 524 fourth-grade public school students (54 percent girls, 46 percent boys) from three geographically distinct regions in Maryland (38.6 percent urban, 30.7 percent suburban, 30.7 percent rural). Of the total sample, 60.7 percent (318 students) were white, 30.9 percent (162 students) were African American, 3.4 percent (18 students) were Hispanic, 2.1 percent (11 students) were Asian or Pacific Islander, and 2.9 percent (15 students) were of some other ethnic background. Approximately 39 percent of the students were from an urban setting, and the other two geographic locations were equally represented (30.7 percent of students were from suburban Maryland; 30.7 percent were from rural Maryland).

The researchers used silhouettes of children to test their sample's body image perception. The pictorials consisted of images of girls and boys, numbered 1 to 7, to correspond with increases in size from very thin to obese. The fourth graders were asked to select images that most looked like the (current body image) and that looked the way they wanted to look (ideal body image). A body image discrepancy score was calculated by subtracting the number of the silhouettes chosen as having the ideal body image from the number of the silhouettes chosen as reflecting the students' current body image. These scores were then sorted into three categories: (1) Participant desires to be thinner (discrepancy scores greater than zero); (2) Participant is satisfied with current image (discrepancy scores equal to zero); and (3) Participant desires to be bigger (discrepancy scores less than zero).

The researchers found that current body image scores did not differ significantly for boys and girls. However, boys had a significantly larger ideal image than girls. Approximately 47 percent of the fourth graders were satisfied with their current image, while the others wanted to be either smaller (42 percent) or larger (11 percent). Urban children had a higher ideal image than their suburban and rural counterparts. Additionally, more children from rural areas (47.2 percent) wanted to lose weight than did children from urban areas (38.6 percent).

Most important, the study found that African American students had significantly higher current image and ideal image scores than did white students and students of other race or ethnicity. In other words, African American fourth graders selected significantly larger figures to represent their current and ideal images than did white, Hispanic, Asian/Pacific Islander, and other students.

Overall, the research team suggests that their study highlights the fact that body image preferences are formed early in life. Caregivers, educators, and health professionals therefore must be mindful of the messages they send young children. Dietitians in particular, by using culturally appropriate materials, can educate both young people and adults about healthy weight, nutrition, exercise, and body image.

Body Image in Middle and High School

In "Body Image and Weight Concerns Among African American and White Adolescent Females: Differences That Make a Difference," [Sheila] Parker et al. examined body image and dieting behaviors among African American and white adolescent females. They explored specifically the cultural factors that have an impact on weight perception, body image, beauty, and style.

In this study, 250 eighth-grade (junior high) and ninth-grade (senior high school) girls were recruited. Informants were 75 percent white, 16 percent Mexican American, and 9 percent Asian American. In the final year of the project, a second sample of forty-six African American adolescent girls, drawn from grades nine through twelve and from various community groups in the same city, was added to the study. The researchers' study of African American adolescent girls utilized both ethnographic interview and survey methods. Ten focus group discussions with four to five girls per group were conducted by African American researchers in order to identify the perceptions and concerns of African American girls regarding their weight and body image, dieting, and other, broader health and lifestyle matters.

The research team consisted of both white and African American researchers. Focus group and individual interviews were transcribed, read, and discussed by members of the research team. Cultural differences and similarities that emerged from the data were analyzed in weekly meetings among the researchers. Later, a panel of community members was asked to comment on the findings.

The researchers stated that what was particularly striking in African American girls' descriptions, when compared with those of white adolescents, was the de-emphasis on external beauty as a prerequisite for popularity. As one girl noted:

> There's a difference between being just fine or being just pretty . . . because I know a lot of girls who aren't just drop-

> dead fine but they are pretty, and they're funny, all those things come in and that makes the person beautiful. There are a lot of bad-looking [physically beautiful] girls out there, but you can't stand being around them.

The researchers also stated that girls were aware that African American boys had more specific physical criteria for the "ideal girl" than what they had themselves. They commented that boys like girls who are shapely, "thick," and who have "nice thighs." One girl noted that "girls would be talkin' about the butt . . . it be big."

Another girl explained the following:

> I think pretty matters more to guys than to me. I don't care. Just real easy to talk to, that would be the ideal girl for me, but the ideal girl from the guy's perspective would be entirely different. They want them to be fine, you know what guys like, shapely. Black guys like black girls who are thick—full-figured.

What was particularly striking in African American girls' descriptions, when compared with those of white adolescents, was the de-emphasis on external beauty as a prerequisite for popularity.

As for the issue of beauty, the researchers found that it was not described in relation to a particular size or set of body statistics. Girls noted that beauty was not merely a question of shape. It was more to be beautiful on the inside as well as on the outside, and to be beautiful a girl had to "know her culture." One girl explained that "African American girls have an inner beauty that they carry within them—their sense of pride." This sense of pride was commonly described as a legacy they received from their mothers.

Overall, the researchers stated that from their study, the standards for body image and beauty among these African

American adolescents could be summed up in what these girls term "looking good." "Looking good"—or "got it goin' on"—expresses the ability of the girl to make whatever it is that she has work for her by creating and presenting a sense of style.

Body Image in College

A study conducted by M. Altabe surveyed 150 male and 185 female college students attending the University of South Florida. Participants completed four different body image questionnaires and several self-ratings that included physical attractiveness and physical appearance scored on a scale of 1 to 11.

Qualitative results from the sampled African Americans, Asian Americans, Caucasian Americans, and Hispanic Americans revealed that height was valued by all groups. Females in all the groups and the Asian and Caucasian males wanted to be thinner. Males in all the groups and the African American and Caucasian females wanted to be more toned. Non-Caucassian females wanted longer hair. All groups valued dark skin or wanted darker skin, except for African American females and Asian males.

African American women rated themselves significantly higher on Sexual Attractiveness than did European American women.

For general appearance body image, African Americans had the most positive self-view. Asian Americans placed the least importance on physical appearance. Thus ethnic differences occurred for both the weight and non-weight dimensions of body image.

Another study on the body image of college-age subjects, titled "Comparison of Body Image Dimensions by Race/Ethnicity and Gender in a University Population," had three major objectives: (1) to examine the interaction of gender and race or ethnicity on body image dimensions, including three racial or ethnic groups in the sample; (2) to more comprehensively measure body image by assessing feelings about body parts significant to race or ethnicity; (3) to measure and control for numerous important possible factors including age, body size, SES, and social desirability.

Participants were 120 college students from a northeastern (n = 27) and a southwestern (n = 93) university. The sample comprised twenty male and twenty female students in each of the three racial or ethnic groups (African American, European American, and Latino American). At the northeastern university, students were recruited from fourteen graduate or undergraduate classes in nine departments, with the permission of the instructors. At the southwestern university, participants were solicited through the research pool (primarily undergraduates) of the Department of Psychology, and were given class credit for their participation.

The researchers found that African Americans scored significantly higher than European Americans and Latino Americans on the dimensions of Appearance Evaluation and Body Areas Satisfaction, and scored above European Americans on the Body Esteem Scale (BES). On the other appearance dimensions, African American women rated themselves significantly higher on Sexual Attractiveness than did European American women, and Latinas scored in the middle. African American women also scored higher than other women on BES dimension of Weight Concern, showing a higher sense of self-esteem regarding their weight. The men did not differ by racial/ethnic group on the BES.

Overall, the researchers suggest that their study helps to expand the database on differences and similarities in body image, based on gender and race or ethnicity. The study makes evident the need to expand the variables under consideration and to place them within a relevant cultural context in an understanding of identity, self-esteem, and self-care.

Body Image Among Professional Adults

A study titled "Does Ethnicity Influence Body Size Preference? A Comparison of Body Image and Body Size" examined body image and body size assessments in a large sample of men and women of four ethnic groups (Hispanic, African American, Asian, and white). The researchers hypothesized that African American women and men would report less body dissatisfaction than the other ethnic groups; that African American and Hispanic men and women, compared with Asians and whites, would accept heavier female figures and would select larger sizes as representing overweight and obesity in females (i.e., would have higher thresholds for what they consider obesity); that regardless of ethnicity, women would be more dissatisfied with their size and shape than men; and that women, compared with men, would select thinner female figures as attractive and acceptable.

From this study of 1,229 participants (801 women and 428 men), of which 288 were Asian, 548 were Hispanic, 208 were African American, and 185 were white, the researchers found that Asian women chose a somewhat larger female figure as being underweight than did African American women; and that Asian women reported less body dissatisfaction than the other groups. In terms of the interaction between gender and race, white women chose the thinnest and African American men chose the heaviest female figure as attractive to men.

In summary, this study investigated body image and the perception of attractive, acceptable, and typical female figures, across a range of sizes from underweight to obese, in a large community sample of Asian, African American, Hispanic, and white men and women. Wide ranges of age, educational level, and BMI were represented, and differences in these variables among groups were controlled. The findings suggested that ethnicity alone does not markedly influence perceptions of female body size. However, cultural acceptance of larger sizes may produce the initial tendency to be overweight. This cultural acceptance of larger sizes directly applies to the African American community.

Another study, "Body Image Preferences Among Urban African Americans and Whites from Low-Income Communities," was conducted to answer two main questions: (1) How do African American and white men and women from similar low-income communities perceive their body mass relative to others in the population? (2) Do ethnic and gender differences exist in the selection of ideal body image sizes for the same and for the opposite sex? Overall, the researchers designed this research as a community study to determine ethnic differences in the relative accuracy of self-estimates of body image and preferences for ideal body image in African American and white low-income communities.

This study was conducted in East Baltimore, Maryland, where adjacent urban African American and white communities of similar low socioeconomic status reside. Nine hundred twenty-seven persons were interviewed during eight weeks and were asked to provide their height and weight and to select body size images from a standardized ethnic group–specific Figure Rating Scale that represented their current self, their ideal self, and their estimation of ideals for the opposite sex. The sample consisted of 579 African Americans (47 percent male, 53 percent female) and 348 whites (46 percent male, 54 percent female).

The researchers found that the average ideal body image for self was the same for African American men and white men, whereas African American women had a significantly greater ideal image compared with white women. Interestingly, the ideal body image for white women was most distant from the image they selected for their current self. Slightly more than one-fourth of white women were satisfied with their current body image, whereas more than half of African American women were satisfied with their current image.

Additionally, the researchers found that African American men indicated a preference for *larger* body images in African American women than did white men for white women. African American women preferred a slightly larger body image for African American men compared with their white counterparts.

In general, the researchers state that their findings support earlier studies in special populations, suggesting that a social norm may exist on a community-wide level that enables the acceptance of larger body images in African American women. Furthermore, this study suggests that there are ethnic differences in body image concepts that necessitate the development of a better appreciation for and understanding of preferred body images and body types in the African American community.

African Americans Need to Feel Good About Larger Body Image

So what conclusion have we derived from this information? The last section of this [viewpoint] presented research studies conducted across the United States in varying age- and school-based categories (in elementary school, in middle and high school, in college, and among professional adults). The studies examined the issues of body image and body preference among African American adults, adolescents, and children and found that African Americans to a significant degree select larger body types as the ideal and for self, as compared to whites. The [viewpoint] began with the contention that African Americans have a "flexible cultural definition of healthiness" that allows us to appreciate, admire, and emulate larger body types as the cultural norm for males and females.

The results of several studies indicate that African Americans have an ideal body type and preference for body image that differ from those of other groups. In fact, we need to keep in mind positive aspects of African American culture that relate to body image, body type, and body preference. This is well stated by [Monica] Baskin, [Harsohena K.] Ahluwalia, and [Ken] Resnicow in their article "Obesity Intervention Among African-American Children and Adolescents":

> Thus, rather than holding whites and majority culture as the ideal, it may be important to incorporate the positive elements of black culture regarding body image and food rather than attempting to shift their values toward those of European Americans.

I wholeheartedly agree with this statement. It is essential that African Americans continue to feel good about our appearance and continue to base our body image within our own culture. Such affirmation will empower us to mentally and physically embrace our individual selves while collectively embracing ourselves as a people.

VIEWPOINT 3

In the United States, Latinas Are Often Caught Between Two Standards of Beauty

Rosie Molinary

A Puerto Rican American herself, Rosie Molinary was interested in the experiences of Latina women who grew up in the United States. She conducted online and telephone surveys of more than five hundred women to find out what they thought. In the following viewpoint, Molinary discusses the challenges Latinas face when confronted with both American ideas about body image and those of their parents' culture, which are usually different. She also talks about how Latinas are represented in the media. Molinary is a teacher and author of Hijas Americanas: Beauty, Body Image, and Growing Up Latina, *from which this viewpoint is excerpted.*

As you read, consider the following questions:

1. What features does the author say made Jennifer Lopez the poster girl for Latina beauty?
2. How do some people say Jennifer Lopez has changed since her early television role as a Fly Girl?
3. According to Molinary's research, what are two different opinions women have about how American values have been internalized by Latinas?

Rosie Molinary, *Hijas Americanas: Beauty, Body Image, and Growing Up Latina*, Cambridge, MA: Seal Press, 2007, pp. 181–192.

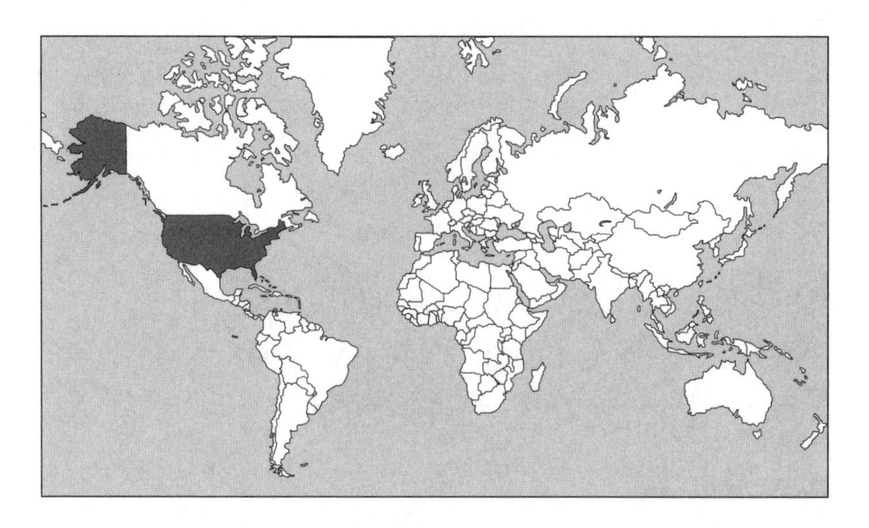

What does it mean to be beautiful in America? The answer to this question brings up all kinds of clichés. Reality shows, magazines, sitcoms, movies, and music videos propagate a certain image—tall, thin, and blonde—that's unattainable for most women. But pop culture isn't the only place where beauty matters. Female news anchors, executives, and CEOs [chief executive officers], even high-power board members, find that beauty plays a role in breaking through the glass ceiling. Beauty is so valued, it's become a commodity.

The question that comes up for me when I think about the power beauty has over our lives and experiences is this: What happens to girls whose self-image is shaped by other people's beauty standards, and whose own features aren't reflected back to them in the everyday images the media promotes? For today's young Latinas, there are some Latina role models, but most of those role models represent yet another unattainable beauty standard. Many Latinas live with a feeling of not being accepted because of how they look. For those of us who have dark skin, raven hair, and a short stature, there isn't much external validation. The average woman of any ethnicity is different from what's celebrated on television, in magazines, and in life. But often, in Latin culture, these differences are exacerbated by the fact that the families' input offers such a distinct point of view—one that's often at odds with the larger culture.

Thus, as Latinas we can be caught in between two standards of beauty—not feeling beautiful in either culture, or feeling beautiful in one but not the other. No matter where we stand, we're on the precipice of judgment, with one set of values that informs our lives shaped by American pop culture and another set shaped by our families' culture and traditions.

Oftentimes there's another perspective as well—our own: a perspective that takes into account the impact of the first two and how they push and pull at our self-image and feelings of who we are. This last perspective is the place where we can find peace in ourselves, which is what ultimately leads us to our real beauty. . . .

As Latinas, we can be caught in between two standards of beauty—not feeling beautiful in either culture, or feeling beautiful in one but not the other. No matter where we stand, we're on the precipice of judgment, with one set of values that informs our lives shaped by American pop culture and another set shaped by our families' culture and traditions.

Latina Actresses Set a Standard for Latina Beauty

When J.Lo [Jennifer Lopez] hit the scene, it seemed that Hollywood suddenly up and took notice of Latinas in a different way. As a Fly Girl on *In Living Color*, her dark, curly hair and strong body reflected her roots. Jenny from the Block was sturdy, not starved. Then, when she played Selena, the slain Chicana singer who was the number-one Latina star in the United States and Mexico before she died, she was introduced to a much broader audience because of the number and diversity of Latinas who flocked to see her on the silver screen.

Soon Jennifer Lopez had caught our collective imagination. She exemplified the modern Latina, but it wouldn't be long before her urban Bronx edge was traded in for a more sophisticated image that turned her into a national—not just Latina—beauty icon. Still, the attention she was getting affirmed Latinas all over the country. Suddenly there was someone who looked a lot more like one of us than the standard blonde beauties of the 1980s and most of the '90s. She became the poster girl for Latina beauty: olive skin, full butt, feminine curves. It wasn't long before other Latinas entered the scene: Eva Mendes, Michelle Rodriguez, Zoe Saldana, Eva Longoria.

In the Growing Up Latina Survey, respondents were asked to list in rank order up to five well-known women of any ethnicity whom they considered beautiful. Eleven of the fifteen top choices reflected women of color. Only two were blondes, which reflects the fact that Hollywood does have many more minority and women-of-color role models than it did fifteen or even ten years ago. The top fifteen women from the survey, in order, were: Salma Hayek, Halle Berry, Angelina Jolie, Jennifer Lopez, Eva Mendes, Catherine Zeta-Jones, Eva Longoria, Beyoncé Knowles, Talisa Soto, Charlize Theron, Jessica Alba, Penélope Cruz, Scarlett Johansson, Adriana Lima, and Tyra Banks.

More and more, women of color, and Latinas specifically, are gracing the covers of magazines, acting as spokeswomen for beauty products, and starring in major motion pictures and television dramas. Beauty in the new millennium, it seems, is diversifying, and the women interviewed for this book have certainly noticed the change.

"Being a Latina has become more mainstream and acceptable, so we're popular right now," says thirty-two-year-old Mia, a Puerto Rican who lives in New York City. "In the media there is more exposure for Latinas, because we're becoming a fad in American mainstream culture. You certainly see more Latinas than when I was growing up."

More and more, women of color, and Latinas specifically, are gracing the covers of magazines, acting as spokeswomen for beauty products, and starring in major motion pictures and television dramas.

Thirty-four-year-old Claudia, who's of Ecuadorian descent and lives in New York, says she felt better as soon as J.Lo entered the public scene. "I grew up with a complex about my body, because I was pretty thick. I always considered myself fat based on what I saw as the perfect American girl. Watching TV and looking at magazines, you see these skinny girls. I used to wear baggy clothes because I felt fat. But once people like J.Lo came out, I started to feel better about my body."

Camille, a twenty-seven-year-old New Yorker who's of mixed Colombian and Dominican descent, agrees with this sentiment. "I just never saw many women like me on the TV when I was growing up. Now I am seeing more women who look like me, and I am making a connection. But when I was growing up, I wanted light eyes and a different body type."

Still, the diversification of the type of women being represented in pop culture and by the media has not completely alleviated the pressure that many Latinas feel about their bodies and looks.

"The media has had a huge, huge impact on what I see as 'pretty.' I am okay with myself, but when I am around other college girls, and they all look like what the media show, I am uncomfortable," says eighteen-year-old Nora, who's *puertorriqueña*, grew up in Charlotte, North Carolina, and feels pressured by American pop culture to have big breasts and a small stomach. "It is all about the body. You don't even have to have a pretty face as long as you have the body."

You would think that the greater representation of Latinas on the small screen and the silver screen would reinvigorate the confidence of Latinas across the country. It's not that easy. Some protest how these women are presented and the implications those portrayals have on the women who are out in mainstream society on a daily basis.

I have always marveled at how the mainstream media praise Latina actresses like Salma Hayek and J.Lo for embracing their curves—but compared to many, these are relatively petite women.

Twenty-five-year-old Gabriela is of Colombian and Cuban descent and is from Houston, Texas. "On the one hand, they portray [Latinas] as hoochies, but on the other hand, they are the fiery and sexy characters who bring a *boom!* to the screen. You have your Salma Hayeks and J.Los, but they are thinner and different from other Latinas," she says.

I agree with Gabriela's observation. I have always marveled at how the mainstream media praise Latina actresses like Salma Hayek and J.Lo for embracing their curves—but compared to many, these are relatively petite women. Salma and J.Lo may have curves, but their bodies are far closer to the bodies of Hollywood's other "It" women than to the average girl on the street in middle America.

Many of the women I interviewed lamented the lack of diversity among the Latinas in Hollywood. "Hollywood doesn't have enough diversity of Latinas. I haven't seen a Latina with cocoa-brown skin and black hair," observed Yvonne, thirty-three, who's Puerto Rican and now lives in Charlotte, North Carolina.

There are Afro-Latina actresses, but many play black characters rather than Latina characters, like Zoe Saldana in the movie *Guess Who?* and Gina Torres of the *Matrix* movies. However, there is an exception: Gina did land a part playing a

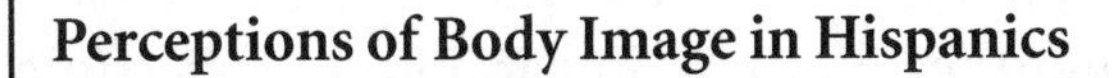

Perceptions of Body Image in Hispanics

Hispanic children's perception of their ideal body size as thinner, the same as, or heavier than their actual body size.

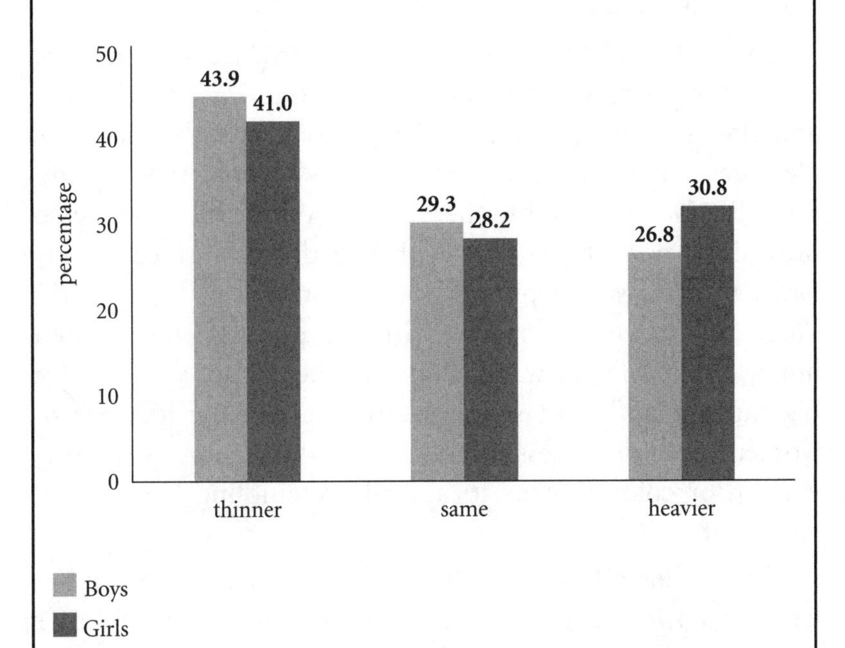

TAKEN FROM: Norma Olvera, Richard Suminski and Thomas G. Power, "Intergenerational Perceptions of Body Image in Hispanics: Role of BMI, Gender, and Acculturation," *Obesity Research*, 2005.

Cuban, her true nationality, when she fast-talked the directors of *Alias* into giving her a role they had intended for a Russian or Czech character. Thus, Anna Espinosa was born, showing prime time television audiences that Latinas come in more than one shade.

While J.Lo is often praised by the media for staying true to her roots, others would argue that she's been altering herself little by little—her hair, her look, her attitude—since her days as a Fly Girl.

"Everything you see on TV, it's not who we are. The Latinas are very thin, and they all look similar. J.Lo keeps getting lighter. Her hair keeps getting straighter," says thirty-three-year-old Mariselle, who's Puerto Rican and Dominican and grew up in Brooklyn.

In the fall of 2006, Jennifer Lopez darkened her hair just before the Toronto Film Festival. The following day, before-and-after photos appeared on People.com with the write-up: "Jennifer Lopez unveiled a radical new look at the Toronto Film Festival last night—her hair is now a deep espresso brown! We haven't seen J.Lo with hair this dark since her Fly Girl days. Was she inspired by all the other stars going dark? We're so used to seeing her with her perfectly highlighted honey-colored locks, we're a little in shock! But we give it a big thumbs up." It's fascinating that despite the increase of women-of-color actresses, it's still breaking news when one woman of color returns to a shade resembling her natural hair color.

People then asked its readers to voice their opinions on her new shade. Responses varied from comments that it better suited her skin tone and made her look younger, to one person who wrote in saying that when Latinas go lighter than their natural hair color, they just look fake. The reaction to J.Lo's hair color says something positive to me: that the diversification within the United States and its media is having an affirmative effect on what people see as viable beauty options. And this is good news for everyone. If mainstream media began embracing women of various sizes and statures, perhaps it would not be long before those images also influenced what we consider to be beautiful in regard to body shape and size.

Clara lives in New York City, and she offers another analysis of Hollywood and J.Lo. She's twenty-nine and part Peruvian, and she opines, "I don't think we even had a voice until J.Lo's butt came along, and suddenly we're getting some recognition that Latina women have butts because white women don't. But J.Lo really made a name for herself with her body, and I think that's sad, because Salma sometimes gets overlooked—and she's an amazing actress."

Reactions to Lopez's acting have alternated between praise for her performance in movies like *Selena* and *Out of Sight* and criticism for films like *Anaconda* and *Gigli*. Yet reviews have consistently called her ravishing and beautiful, and her looks are rarely overlooked in a critique of her performance. The way Latina actresses are scrutinized for their appearance is telling about what critics value and what they believe Latinas are bringing to the screen.

It's not just stereotypes about looks that critics play into. Stereotypes about the "Latina character" are featured, too. In 2006, in a review of the play *Torches*, which ran in Charlotte, North Carolina, a male reviewer wrote of a Latina actress: "After years of mostly forgettable performances in and around Charlotte, [she] seems to be tapping into her inner Latina. In quick succession, she has sizzled in two hot-blooded roles." Seriously?

One survey respondent wrote that she felt that Latina actresses were still viewed in a marginalized way. "Famous Latinas are not celebrated on the same level as other actresses. They are just considered beautiful for their slender and exotic looks."

Other survey participants worried about the implications of how Latinas are portrayed. One respondent wrote, "Most of these women are portrayed in sexual roles. The most famous Latinas in America are movie stars, which may cause Americans to think that we do not have any Latina women who are famous for other successes, such as politics, writing, social movements, for being community leaders, et cetera. I do feel that some of these women, like Salma Hayek, have done a great job at being educated about societal problems, and not just for being pretty faces."

"It's somewhat sad," says Jessica, a twenty-two-year-old Chicago student of El Salvadoran descent, describing the way Hollywood portrays Latinas. "We are rowdy, rambunctious women—uneducated, speak with a slight accent, with big butts—who dance merengue. The Latinas who've made it are from specific backgrounds, like Mexico and Puerto Rico, and they're closing the public's eye to all the differences of Latinos and Latino culture."

Pop culture movements are dramatically affecting young Latinas in the United States. One such movement is Reggaetón, a musical craze that's a hybrid of different music and cultures.

"Young people are desperate for identity. I see this a lot in the girls that I advise," says Gloria, age forty and born in Puerto Rico. She now mentors young Latinas in New Jersey. "They have this whole thing in trying to identify with the image that Reggaetón promotes. It is the big charms, the big pants, the slang. This doesn't make you Puerto Rican. I think it's really sad where things are heading. Latinos have a lot more representation on TV, but there is a stereotype going around because of Reggaetón and movies and videos that show Latinos as streetwise. This is what the young kids identify as being Latino."

I know that not having Latina role models when I was growing up was difficult, but sometimes I wonder whether it's even harder for Latinas growing up today, because the Latina role models on display are really in a league of their own.

As Latinas, we're inevitably shaped by the images we see, but we can choose whether and how we internalize these values. In my research, women's opinions ranged widely. Some felt that American culture has truly made progress based on the mere fact that there are so many more Latinas in the mainstream media than there were five years ago. Others felt that we are still marginalized, and the very notion of lifting up these few women is equivalent to treating them like tokens, or poster girls, for Latinas as a whole.

Me? I fall somewhere in between: I'm thrilled to see the diversity that exists in the world begin to take root in American media, but sometimes I'm mortified by things like the choice of title for the ABC telenovela *Ugly Betty*. I know it's meant to be sarcastic and ironic, since Betty is the most together, well-intentioned, and good-humored character on the show. It might even be a clarion call for us about how we see beauty. But there is still a poignancy about calling her ugly, naming an anxiety that's so acute. To me, it seems to speak to the fact that plenty of people don't flinch at calling women ugly, fat, and many other descriptors that are direct attacks on our physical appearances. What are we saying to young girls when we identify someone as ugly just because she has bad hair, braces, and glasses?

I know that not having Latina role models when I was growing up was difficult, but sometimes I wonder whether it's even harder for Latinas growing up today, because the Latina role models on display are really in a league of their own. For a while it seemed as though Latina role models were far underrepresented compared to the range of female African American role models who were becoming more visible: Black girls had Queen Latifah, Aisha Tyler, Halle Berry, Beyoncé [Knowles], Kerry Washington, and Janet Jackson long before any real Latina presence could be seen in the media. Fortunately, women like America Ferrera are showing us a more representative view of Latina women. Her work in *Real Women Have Curves* and *The Sisterhood of the Traveling Pants* revealed the depth of the Latina experience.

Sara Ramírez's role as Dr. Callie Torres on *Grey's Anatomy* portrays a strong, smart, beautiful, and average-size Latina. And it works, except for the occasional script misstep, such as the scene where another doctor describes her as so sexy that she is "dirty sexy." Why does the Latina doctor have to be the one who's *dirty* sexy?

VIEWPOINT 4

The Western Media Influence Perceptions of Body Image

Shari Graydon

In this viewpoint, Canadian author Shari Graydon discusses how the images of women presented by the media influence women's perceptions of their own bodies. She describes the heavily promoted makeover industry as well as the preponderance of underweight models, both of which cause women to be dissatisfied with their own bodies. She also suggests some ways that women can respond to these media portrayals.

As you read, consider the following questions:

1. What did fashion shows in Milan and Madrid do to help discourage the use of extremely thin models?
2. How do academic studies say that women are impacted by exposure to unrealistically thin and beautiful models?
3. What do media literacy programs in schools do, as described by the author?

The rap sheet gets longer every year—spend five minutes in the slow line at your local supermarket checkout and you can't avoid being reminded of the heinous nature of crimes against women's body image.

"Janet Jackson's shocking weight gain!" scream the headlines; "Jennifer Love Hewitt's butt is enormous!" and "Posh has dimpled legs!"

Shari Graydon, "How the Media Keeps Us Hung Up on Body Image," *Herizons*, vol. 22, Summer 2008, pp. 17–19.

Fortunately, help is at hand, often within the very same publications. Not coincidentally, they promise "Foods that erase belly fat!" and "Professional trainer's tips to get bikini-ready!"

After decades of feminist activism and enlightenment, how is it "we're still here?" Strange, but true, the cautionary words of Dwight Eisenhower provide an instructive parallel. In 1960, with a perceptiveness that eluded him in office, the outgoing U.S. president "warned," "we must guard against the acquisition of unwarranted influence, whether sought or unsought, by the military-industrial complex."

Substitute "makeover-industry culture" for "military-industrial complex" and you get the same "disastrous rise of misplaced power" Eisenhower cautioned against. And, just as America's dedication of resources to military operations has grown significantly in recent decades, so has there been a veritable explosion in the number of commercial enterprises with a vested financial interest in ensuring that women and girls are more at war with their bodies than ever before.

Consider that in 2008 the legion of aggressively promoted makeover solutions to remedy our failure to live up to feminine ideals has gone far beyond mere cosmetics, exercise regimes and diet programs. The fixes now on offer include liposuction, stomach stapling, anti-cellulite creams, breast, butt, cheek and chin implants, Botox and collagen injections, chemical peels, facelifts and labia surgery.

Complications from Plastic Surgery Have Caused Deaths

The list is heart-stopping—sometimes literally. At least three prominent women have died in recent years from complications from plastic surgery: Olivia Goldsmith, the American fiction writer who penned *The First Wives Club*, Micheline Charest, a prominent Quebec communications executive; and Donda West, the mother of popular hip-hop artist Kanye

West. No doubt others have, too. They just haven't made headlines, because without the celebrity connection the news would be merely tragic, as opposed to titillating.

Given the advent of size-zero fashions, and, with television series such as *Extreme Makeover* and *The Swan* promoting surgery as a means of achieving the impossible, such deaths aren't surprising. But when even the teenagers and twenty-somethings actually blessed with skinny genes are collapsing from starvation on fashion runways, the damage being caused by the cultural normalization of "extreme" is undeniable.

The French have always claimed one must suffer to be beautiful, but you're forgiven for believing that obscenely premature death may actually defeat the purpose.

In search of a contemporary trend to feel good about, it was tempting last year [2007] to celebrate the fact that fashion shows in Milan and Madrid imposed a minimum body mass index (height/weight fat ratio) on the female models they hired. The British Fashion Council declined to establish a minimum BMI [body mass index], but announced that it recognized its "responsibility" and had asked its designers to use only "healthy" models aged 16 or older.

Unfortunately, all these industry responses were belated reactions to the public outrage that greeted two highly publicized deaths. In August 2006, Uruguayan model Luisel Ramos starved herself for her career and was rewarded with heart failure that killed her at the age of 22. Three months later, her 21-year-old Brazilian colleague Ana Carolina Reston also died of complications resulting from anorexia.

The French have always claimed one must suffer to be beautiful, but you're forgiven for believing that obscenely premature death may actually defeat the purpose. Insisting that models conform to a minimum body mass index is also not a progressive solution.

Merryl Bear, director of the National Eating Disorder Information Centre, calls the move "completely disingenuous. The fashion industry has downloaded responsibility to the very people who have the least power," she says. "Models are at the bottom of the food chain."

At the top are the designers, photographers and editors who continue to deny the political context altogether, maintaining that their preferred slim physiques are merely an aesthetic choice, fuelled by the perception that clothes drape better on bodies that resemble wire coat hangers.

Media Distract Women from Focusing on What Bodies Do

Unfortunately, that aesthetic has helped to drive a multibillion-dollar industry that thrives by distracting women away from a focus on what our bodies do, overwhelming us instead with images of how they ought to look. The result is that, compared to our sisters of a generation ago, women today have an unprecedented number of opportunities to judge themselves against a select and genetically freakish few.

It's true that Twiggy inspired some serious dieting behaviour in her day. But the iconic waif was neither ubiquitous nor replicated by dozens of high-profile imitators. Today, in contrast, stars like Lindsay Lohan, Nicole Richie, Paris Hilton, Mischa Barton and Mary-Kate Olsen are regularly celebrated and condemned alike for what, in a neonatal ward, would be termed "failure to thrive." In fact, the voracious tabloids have ensured that their performances on the consumption stage (eat normally or walk the red carpet with pride—you decide) have largely eclipsed whatever artistic talents originally made them famous.

Yesteryear's magazine racks sported exponentially fewer publications devoted to fame voyeurism and advising women on the finer points of dressing up, dressing down or sculpting our bodies in pursuit of a profile that we'd be happy to avoid dressing altogether. *Cosmo* and *Vogue* are now buried under a deluge of other fashion and "fitness" magazines, while a host of new titles supplement the print lessons available to male readers regarding what's "desirable" and "ideal" when it comes to the sizes and shapes of women's body parts.

Furthermore, the body parts on display have become less and less realistic. In addition to the ubiquitous presence of breast implants, increasingly sophisticated Photoshop technology now permits an unprecedented degree of artificiality in application to hips, thighs, waists, arms and necks. We are reminded of this only occasionally, when someone like Kate Winslet has the temerity to question the aggressive airbrushing that some magazine has used to transform her body into an unrecognizable mannequin.

Models Become Smaller as Real Women Become Larger

Meanwhile, models themselves are becoming smaller, even as real women grow larger. Analyses of the body sizes of *Playboy* centrefolds and Miss America contestants over the years have demonstrated diminishing trends in both cases. Pageant winners have become significantly slimmer and less curvaceous, and almost all of the contemporary centrefolds assessed in a 1999 study were considered underweight in the context of Canadian guidelines. Close to a third met the World Health Organization's BMI criteria for anorexia.

It may be small consolation to know that our depth of understanding about the impact of these images on our emotional, psychological and physical health has improved. Dozens of peer-reviewed academic studies now document the degree of dissatisfaction women and girls experience with themselves after exposure to unrealistically thin and beautiful female models and actors. Indeed, the more time we spend immersed in contemporary media, the more likely we are to obsess about our appearance or develop disordered eating behaviour.

Quantifying the incidence of eating disorders remains a challenge, says Bear, in part because of differing definitions and the dependency of researchers on self-identification. Some studies suggest that the rates of anorexia stabilized in the 1980s, while those of bulimia continue to increase. The affected population is also changing: Many women in midlife who previously had no history of disordered eating now appear to be developing problems.

Media images are never a sufficient condition, of course: many other factors contribute. But it's impossible to deny their reach. Recent research published in the *Canadian Medical Association Journal* found that close to one in three preadolescent girls is trying to lose weight and one in 10 shows symptoms of an eating disorder.

Among younger women and girls, says Bear, eating disorders have the highest mortality rates of all psychiatric disorders. Girls affected are 12 times more likely to die than those who are not, she says, and disordered eating has become the third most chronic illness in adolescence.

Nor should we be encouraged by the migration of young media consumers away from print and TV sources and onto the Internet. The vast storehouses of pornography available on the Net reinforce equally distorted visions, not just of women's bodies but of how they "desire" to be "used." And so far the self-posted images of a new generation of young women who use social networking sites to become media creators as well as consumers suggest the commercial landscape's dominant trends are being replicated more often than they're challenged.

Taking Action for Change

What can we do in response?

On a macro scale, the challenge is as fraught today as it ever was. We're up against individual plastic surgeons and multinational corporations alike, all of whom have a vested interest in continuing to feed the commodification of insecurity. Even the makers of Dove, which won the customer loyalty of millions of women for using images of diverse non-models, remains part of the problem. (Reflecting the cynical self-interest of the industry at large, its parent company Unilever also markets products like Slim-Fast and Fair and Lovely, a skin-whitening agent.)

And yet the explosion of alternative media sources—this magazine [*Herizons*] among them—does give us some options. In 2008 it is possible for individuals to avoid mainstream magazines and TV shows that perpetuate body image trauma while offering news and entertainment. In the process of supporting feminist media producers and promoting the analysis found there, we can also shore up our own resistance to the images' impact when we are exposed.

As Media Watch discovered in the 1990s, it's actually not enough to boycott retrograde companies or even to enroll our friends in joining the fight. We actually have to let the manufacturers, advertisers, publishers, and programmers know that they're losing business by behaving in unethical and destructive ways.

Media literacy programs in schools provide similar protection for young people. Teaching critical thinking in application to how media industries work, how media images are constructed and why—nurtures kids' skepticism and gives them some capacity to challenge the implicit and explicit claims made.

Changing the pictures themselves is much more difficult. We can hope the resonance achieved by the Dove campaign signals that the pendulum has swung as far into artifice as it can and is now poised to drift back into the authenticity zone. Or we can help it along by mobilizing our networks to deliver messages about consumer dissatisfaction to the people and companies responsible for the creation and dissemination of unhealthy, destructive images.

We know this is important, though few of us actually take the time to do it. But as Media Watch discovered in the 1990s, it's actually not enough to boycott retrograde companies or even to enroll our friends in joining the fight. We actually have to let the manufacturers, advertisers, publishers and programmers know that they're losing business by behaving in unethical and destructive ways. In the process, we might inform them of recent British research finding that skinny models aren't any more effective at selling products than regular-sized women, and encourage them to capitalize on the real-women trend spearheaded by Dove.

The tactics may seem laughably inadequate to the task of toppling the mammoth makeover industry culture, but at very least, by engaging in such manoeuvres, we'll be directing our firepower at the real enemy, and away from our own perfect reflections in the mirror.

VIEWPOINT 5

Measuring the Ideal Female Figure

Martin Gruendl

The Department of Psychology at the University of Regensburg, Germany, is conducting an ongoing online research project that surveys people's views of the ideal female body by having them alter the dimensions of a computer-generated drawing of a woman. In this viewpoint Martin Gruendl, chair of the Department of Experimental Psychology, discusses how the ideal body image has changed over time and how it has stayed the same. He also describes some other research that has been done on the topic.

As you read, consider the following questions:

1. What does Gruendl say about the ideal waist-to-hip ratio?
2. What did researcher Devendra Singh discover Miss America contestants and *Playboy* models have in common?
3. What does the author say women do to change the distribution of body fat with which they were born?

What actually determines an attractive women's figure? For most people the answer is absolutely clear: An attractive woman must be above all slender. It is no wonder

Martin Gruendl, "Beautiful Figure," Beauty Check, 2007. Reproduced by permission. www.beautycheck.de.

then, most women judge themselves as being too big and are not content with their own figure. Although this ideal of attractiveness seems natural to us, historically seen, this ideal is new and unique.

The Modern Slimness Ideal

Before the beginning of the 20th century, most women who were considered to be attractive had bodies richly equipped with typically feminine curves. For instance much quoted "Rubens women" [referring to women portrayed in the works of artist Peter Paul Rubens] are an extreme example which portrays women not only consistent with the social trend at that time, but most likely reflected the personal taste of the painter. A glance at the paintings and sculptures of the old masters clearly shows that for centuries feminine figures which were once considered to be appealing, would be regarded today as being too fat.

Researchers have stated that in former times the ideal of attractiveness, or being fat, was considered to be a status symbol. Only the well-to-do could afford to eat well, while the poor remained slender from lack of food. However today, the supply of food is abundant and fat has lost its value of information as a sign of prosperity. To a certain extent, this correlation has reversed: For instance in the US [United States] obesity has become a problem of the lower class.

If the preference of slimness has something to do with economic prosperity, people should then prefer fatter bodies in economically poorer countries. And thus it is. A worldwide study in which 62 different cultures were examined showed that being slim is preferred above all in countries where people do not think twice about their daily bread. In poor countries, however, heavier women are judged as being more beautiful.

Also the social position of the woman seems to play a role in body size: In traditional cultures where women are primarily housewives and mothers, more corpulent figures are preferred. In cultures where women have more political power and more economic participation and employment, slender figures are preferred. . . . [Researchers showed in the 20th century] this connection also existed in the Western world. The more traditional the women's role, the more curvaceous was the ideal figure. The greater the economic growth and the women's role in the educational system and employment, the less curvaceous was the ideal body.

A worldwide study in which 62 different cultures were examined showed that being slim is preferred above all in countries where people do not think twice about their daily bread. In poor countries, however, heavier women are judged as being more beautiful.

The Ideal Waist-to-Hip Ratio Remains Relatively Constant

However, the ideal figure is not completely dependent on social influence, but rather derived from a numerical ratio, namely the waist-to-hip ratio (WHR). It does not matter whether a person is fat or slender, the ideal relation should approximate 0.7. This value is calculated by dividing the waist circumference by the hip circumference. Example: 63 cm of waist circumference by 90 cm of hip circumference which makes 0.7.

The WHR is gender specific. Women tend to have a lower WHR compared to men. Until the beginning of puberty, the relationship between waist and hip is almost identical in boys and girls (nearly 0.9). Later the influence of estrogen causes the pelvis to grow in women. This results in the typical female fat distribution where fat accumulates in the buttocks and upper thighs, causing the WHR to deviate from 0.7. In males the hip in proportion to waist remains small (the ideal is here 0.9).

Devendra Singh, researcher specializing in attractiveness, carried out numerous investigations in the waist-to-hip ratio in the nineties. He discovered that all winners of the "Miss America contests" from 1920 until the 1980s had a WHR between 0.72 and 0.69. He also found that *Playboy* models' WHR was between 0.71 and 0.68. For decades the ideal waist-to-hip ratio was consistently 0.7, despite the changing body weight of these models. Thus, in spite of their different weight classes, the beauty icons Marilyn Monroe, Sophia Loren, Twiggy and Kate Moss all had at least one thing in common—a WHR of about 0.7.

However, it is not so simple. Recent investigations have questioned the validity of the magic 0.7. In non-westernized cultures the preferred WHR is roughly 0.9 (in the direction of male proportions).

For decades the ideal waist-to-hip ratio [WHR] was consistently 0.7, despite the changing body weight of these models. Thus, in spite of their different weight classes, the beauty icons Marilyn Monroe, Sophia Loren, Twiggy and Kate Moss all had at least one thing in common—a WHR of about 0.7.

Different WHR preferences have also been found in westernized cultures. While in the middle ages a more corpulent waist was in vogue, the renaissance and baroque eras brought popularity to the hourglass figure. It was additionally emphasized by clothing such as corsets and crinolines.

In the 1920s, boy-like figures were popular among women and the feminine waist was concealed by loosely fitting clothes. In the 1950s the "WASP's waist" was desired.

In addition, the methodology for obtaining the results of the waist-to-hip ratio has been criticized. In most experiments the change did not focus on the WHR, but rather the altered waist size. If the waist is made smaller, the WHR decreases.

However the ratio would also be reduced if the waist size remained the same but the hip was made wider.

However, it is doubtful whether the experimental subjects would still find a figure with broader hips and normal waist as attractive in contrast to a figure with the same WHR but with a normal hip and narrow waist.

Nevertheless, with the famous experiments of Singh only two variables were changed on the shown female dummies [mannequins]: The corpulence (underweight, normal-weight, overweight) and the waist width (0.7 to 1.0).

Ideal Bust Size Changes over Time

However, there's more to a woman's figure than corpulence, waist and hip. The suitable bust size also belongs to the beauty of a women's figure. However, what suits? It is also worthwhile to review historical preference: In previous centuries an ideal woman's figure emphasized small breasts. At first ideal breasts were small and round—in the middle ages the ideal breasts were compared to apples. Today, however, the ideal figure incorporates a big bust (especially in westernized countries).

It is also fascinating that in previous centuries, the woman needed to be rather youthful-girl-like on top with a graceful bust and with a feminine bottom and upper thighs that were rich in fat. Today, however, the ideal is exactly reversed: Now a great bust is desired and is paired with a narrow, rather of a little bit androgynous hip. The irony of all this, is that back then, like today, both beauty ideals were barely attainable, because they were extremely unrealistic. Either a woman's figure has a great deal of fat and her figure is luxuriant below as well as on top, or she is slender and has narrow hips and slender thighs with small breasts.

Today in contrast to former times, there is the possibility to annul the rule of body fat distribution (either fat everywhere or nowhere) with which we were born. Thus it is not surprising that more and more women "amend" their figures

Obtaining a Perfect Body Is an Endless Heartbreaking Campaign

I have been to more than forty countries in the last six years. I have seen the rampant and insidious poisoning: skin-lightening creams sell as fast as toothpaste in Africa and Asia; the mothers of eight-year-olds in America remove their daughters' ribs so they will not have to worry about dieting; five-year-olds in Manhattan do strict asanas [yoga postures] so they won't embarrass their parents in public by being chubby; girls vomit and starve themselves in China and Fiji and everywhere; Korean women remove Asia from their eyelids . . . the list goes on and on.

I have been in a dialogue with my stomach for the past three years. I have entered my belly—the dark wet underworld—to get at the secrets there. I have talked with women in surgical centers in Beverly Hills; on the sensual beaches of Rio de Janeiro; in the gyms of Mumbai, New York, Moscow; in the hectic and crowded beauty salons of Istanbul, South Africa, and Rome. Except for a rare few, the women I met loathed at least one part of their body. There was almost always one part that they longed to change, that they had a medicine cabinet full of products devoted to transforming or hiding or reducing or straightening or lightening. Just about every woman believed that if she could just get that part right, everything else would work out. Of course, it is an endless heartbreaking campaign.

Eve Ensler, The Good Body.
New York: Random House, 2004, p. xii–xiv.

with the help of surgical breast implants. Also, the trend seems to move towards a fuller bust size, as the implants used during the last several years have become bigger and bigger. A front-runner of this trend is the US and it seems to influence other countries with their beauty ideal, for example in breast size.

Now a great bust is desired and is paired with a narrow, rather of a little bit androgynous hip.

In Brazil, for instance, women traditionally had a curvaceous pelvis, a fuller bottom and a small bust. They were considered to be beautiful. For Brazilians, large breasts were regarded as vulgar. However, in the last several years the Brazilian beauty ideal has approximated the American ideal, and breast implants in Brazil have become larger.

Long Legs Are Also a Factor in a Beautiful Figure

The last important feature of a beautiful woman's figure is long legs. It's actually quite obvious, since legs have been artificially lengthened for decades by high heel shoes. However, although this criteria is important for the general public, up until now, it has rarely been examined in research dealing with attractiveness. Singh's investigations did not include legs as a factor and simply faded out this important variable.

In our online experiments dealing with the ideal female figure, we have taken into consideration all five mentioned variables: Corpulence, pelvic width, waist width, bust size and leg length. Each feature of our stimulus material exists in three variations (e.g., broad—middle—narrow), and all variations are combinable independently of each other—therefore, there are 243 possible combinations (3 x 3 x 3 x 3 x 3 = 243). Also, we did not use outline drawings, but rather photo material which we have changed with the help of morphing software. The online experiments of the University of Regensburg are unique because of the realistic nature and variety of the stimulus material and are now available worldwide.

We expect to receive more exact knowledge from the data regarding the ideal figure rather the different ideal figure of different societies. The first results suggest that there are different ideal types depending on the observer.

Viewpoint 6

Worldwide Beauty Contests

Rosie Goldsmith

BBC reporter Rosie Goldsmith traveled around the world studying beauty pageants. In this viewpoint, she describes beauty pageants she visited in the United States, China, and South Africa, highlighting the commonalities she observed in the pageants and the contestants.

As you read, consider the following questions:

1. What does Goldsmith say about beauty pageants and tourism?
2. When and where was the first modern beauty competition?
3. As described in the viewpoint, what reasons did contestants give for pushing themselves so hard in beauty competitions?

"And you gotta recall, Miss Rosie," Jessica Tucker tells me in her *Ya-Ya Sisterhood* voice, "that this is a scholarship programme and we are all professional ladies." Tucker, Miss Watermelon, is competing in the Miss Louisiana beauty pageant for the fifth time, and "failure" is a dirty word. (They call it "failing forward".) Miss Louisiana is one of the US-wide preliminary state heats for the coveted Miss America, to be held in January 2006. [Miss Louisiana won a $3,000 scholar-

Rosie Goldsmith, "And the Winner Is . . ." *New Statesman*, October 17, 2005, pp. 34–35.

ship in the 2006 Miss America competition.] For this one contest you may train for up to a year, up to 16 hours a day. Tucker is indeed a professional—a qualified electrical engineer. She is also an excellent pianist and has been able to get herself through college with her beauty pageant winnings. The pretty, athletic 22-year-old has been "pageanting" for several years. The reigning Miss Louisiana, I discover, started at 18 months old. "We prime the boys for soccer and baseball, and our daughters for pageants," her doting mum explains. "And here in the South, we *love* our pageants."

Despite Feminist Objections, Beauty Pageants Are Lucrative Around the World

In politically correct Britain, beauty contests are an apologetic, backstreet industry, but they still flourish elsewhere: My beauty odyssey for [BBC] Radio 4 took me from Louisiana in the US to Sun City in South Africa and Hangzhou in China. All the competitions I saw were buoyed by eager corporate and community sponsors and undimmed by feminism, anti-racism and falling TV ratings. Beauty pageants are lucrative for the hotel and restaurant trades, as well as for the beauty and fashion industries. In China, the sole reason given for the enormous, extravagant Miss Tourism Queen International pageant was to promote tourism and "the beauty of China" in the city of Hangzhou, in east China's Zhejiang Province. It was the same story with Miss Louisiana and the Face of Africa in Sun City; beauty as a calling card for tourism. Beauty pageants mirror the state of a nation: its economy, its ambition, its self-image.

The modern beauty competition was born in the US. The world's market leader, the country holds in the region of 3,500 contests a year, from Miss Chicken Drumsticks to the spectacular, lavish, celebrity-driven circuses of Miss America and Miss USA (the latter is part-owned by Donald Trump). Miss America started off in Atlantic City in 1921 as showcase for both beauty and tourism. The first contests were seedy affairs, but they were soon touched by Hollywood glamour and, during the Second World War, became patriotic, respectable and a particularly American form of upward mobility. (It wasn't until 1984, however, that the first black Miss America—Vanessa Williams—was crowned, after decades of protest.)

In China, pageants remain a novelty. After years of official disapproval—in the 1950s, Chairman Mao [Zedong] called them "bourgeois nonsense"—they only really took off in 2003, with the arrival of Miss World in its new home of uncritical capitalism. Today, pageants in China can't be big or brash enough. They are an integral part of the country's huge beauty industry, which is the fourth-largest growth area in China after cars, real estate and tourism. Paul French, a market analyst in Shanghai, observes: "Pageants are a sign that China has arrived on the world stage and can match the US."

In the new multiracial, inclusive South Africa, I was astonished to find there were no white finalists at all in the Face of Africa. The message these days is "black empowerment". The slick and splashy competition was a conscious display of black music, black fashion designers and black beauty—a backlash against the apartheid years, when even beauty contests were segregated.

Beauty pageant finals tend to be vast, frenzied affairs. In nations without royalty, the winners can become queens, elevated and idealised far beyond their often humble beginnings. One Face of Africa hopeful had taken a four-hour bus ride from her village and stood for hours in the baking sun for the auditions.

But why do these women push themselves so hard? The answers were always the same: "To get a better life", "To become a TV star/get a job in fashion", "To travel" and "I'm doing this for my country".

Each of the 30 Miss Louisiana finalists won cash towards college fees, while Miss America 2005, Deidre Downs, received

Pageants May Be Used to Promote Greater Causes

These days beauty contests—a sort of dog-and-pony show—are an anachronism; at worst misogynistic. Pageant organizers reject this, of course. "We're not about beauty queens in bathing suits," Sylvia Stark, director of Miss Canada International, recently told guests at a dinner promoting her event. While beautiful women still parade on stage in evening gowns and cocktail dresses, they do so in a competition for academic scholarships.

The Miss Canada International pageant has reinvented itself as an organization dedicated to public service and ambassadorship (winners are expected to spend a year supporting charitable causes). Miss World, meanwhile, serves up "beauty with a purpose;" Miss Universe advocates HIV awareness; Miss Earth is devoted to the environment.

Zachary Goelman, "There She Is . . . Miss Whatever," Ottawa Citizen *(Canada), May 11, 2009.*

$50,000. In China, the monetary prize is small, but you have the chance to travel and promote tourism. This year's Face of Africa winner, Kaone Kario, received a three-year modelling contract, clothes, free flights, makeup, a holiday, mobile phones: big prizes for any girl.

> *"Being a beauty queen is a job and they have to treat it like training for the Olympics, with discipline."*

So has feminism given up on the beauty contests? Wherever I raised the issue of exploitation, or pornography, or victimisation, people looked at me quizzically. Today's beauty queens were born long after the 1960s when feminists called for pageants to be banned.

"How can you be happy for your daughter to be lusted over in public?" I asked Byron, the Methodist minister father of Katherine Putnam, one of the Louisiana finalist, after watching her scissor-walk across stage in her revealing swimsuit. "That," Byron said, "is the problem for the observer, not for us. Beauty is not evil. Katherine eats well. She works out. She has a healthy body. Those are good things to promote in our society. If she wins, she'd be a role model for others."

At the end of my odyssey I felt I'd been at a month-long wedding: uplifted but rather sick on the excess of glitter and gaiety. The girls were little more than pretty bridesmaids in a big national branding campaign. In South Africa, village girls plucked from obscurity have been launched on the international modelling stage, to become, as one judge told me, "our own African Kate Moss". In China, I found the 70 contestants in Miss Tourism Queen International desperate for the whole shambolic event to end. They'd been travelling through the country as "tourism ambassadors" for nearly a month. They'd lost weight, and their frocks and sashes were grubby. The contest organiser, however, was unsympathetic: "Being a beauty queen is a job and they have to treat it like training for the Olympics, with discipline."

Periodical Bibliography

The following articles have been selected to supplement the diverse views presented in this chapter.

Donna Abu-Nasr — "Beneath Robes and Veils, Saudi Women Get Nips and Tucks," *Jakarta Globe* (Indonesia), August 3, 2009.

Swati Anand — "Beauty's Beast," *Little India*, January 2006. www.littleindia.com.

Fatima Chowdhury — "India: Body Image: Cruel Reflection," Women's Feature Service, November 28, 2007. www.wfsnews.org.

Trisha M. Dunkel, Denise Davidson, and Shaji Qurashi — "Body Satisfaction and Pressure to Be Thin in Younger and Older Muslim and Non-Muslim Women: The Role of Western and Non-Western Dress Preferences," *Body Image*, January 2010.

Steven Gregor — "The Man Behind the Mask: Male Body Image Dissatisfaction," *InPsych*, June 2004.

Shanti Kumar — "Globalisation, Nationalism and Feminism in Indian Culture," *South Asian Journal*, July–September 2004.

Naci Mocan and Erdal Tekin — "Ugly Criminals," *Review of Economics and Statistics*, February 2010.

Taiwo Oloruntoba-Oju — "Body Image, Beauty, Culture and Language in the Nigerian African Context," *Sexuality in Africa*, December 2008.

Marwa Salem — "Plastic Surgery Fever Invades Morocco's Muslim Society," *Jakarta Globe* (Indonesia), August 9, 2009.

CHAPTER 3

Enhancing the Body

VIEWPOINT 1

Men Are Taking More Care to Improve Their Appearances

Lindy Woodhead

Lindy Woodhead has worked in public relations and has written for the fashion industry for more than thirty years. In the following viewpoint, she describes how the men's grooming industry has recently boomed from a few basic toiletries to full-service, male-only salons. She says that more men are recognizing the benefits of being well-groomed and that their skin is fundamentally different from women's skin.

As you read, consider the following questions:

1. In the recent past, what does Woodhead say made up a man's grooming regime?
2. What does the author say happened to start a trend toward more thorough grooming for men?
3. How does the author say many reticent men first start going to male-only salons?

It doesn't surprise me to learn that [British politician] David Cameron sports a sparkling set of buffed—possibly even polished—nails. It's simply another sign of his impeccable modernist credentials.

It doesn't seem so very long ago that a grooming regime for most men involved a razor, a can of shaving foam, a splash of aftershave and a monthly haircut. No more. To the delight of the cosmetic companies, today's urban male is finally scouring the shelves for specialist male-grooming products. The result isn't just smoother skin—it all adds up to a global market value of nearly [pounds sterling] 10 billion each year. There hasn't been as much excitement in the business of male marketing since 1901, when Gillette launched the first safety razor with disposable blades.

Steering the complex pathway to seduce and educate the hearts and minds of the Anglo Saxon 'macho male' hasn't been easy. Most early offerings involved the ubiquitous 'soap on a rope' and waves of Old Spice. Until comparatively recently, even the most skilful of copywriters couldn't persuade men between 30 and 50 to take their skin care seriously. It was the testosterone-fuelled twentysomething who was spending over an hour in the bathroom, showering and scenting to impress his hot date.

To the delight of the cosmetic companies, today's urban male is finally scouring the shelves for specialist male-grooming products.

Then suddenly—as with trends that become mainstream—the lines blurred and a new attitude took hold.

Men Waxing Unwanted Hair

It could be argued it all started with hair.

While [actor] Richard Gere and Bill Clinton have proved it's cool to be grey, [athlete] David Beckham fuelled the trend for the hairless body.

Suddenly, what was on top was of less importance than what lurked beneath, with the result that men have finally realised that there is nothing less appealing, not to mention more ageing, than too much hair in the wrong places.

"Real men have died out . . . there are only softies left! Don't make me cry. My eye shadow could bleed," cartoon by Karsten Schley, www.CartoonStock.com. Copyright © Karsten Schley. Reproduction rights obtainable from www.CartoonStock.com.

The only problem for men failing the magnifying mirror test was how—and where—to get rid of the offending stuff in dignified comfort. Enter the male-only grooming salon.

Leader in the field is the Refinery, which opened [in the United Kingdom] in Mayfair in 2000 and now operates a branch in Bishopsgate and another at Harrods, alongside its Brook Street flagship. Waxing dominates the treatment list, with the most popular parts to be stripped being backs, shoulders and hairy hands. For those brave enough to go further, the Refinery's 'Galaxy'—a wince-inducing waxing of pubic hair—is apparently gaining in popularity. My husband, who happily experimented with several treatments at the Refinery by way of research for this feature, drew the line at the 'Galaxy', so I am unable to confirm if its Australian wax, specially formulated for shorter, coarser male hair, hovers beneath the pain threshold.

Male-Only Salons Are Gaining Popularity

The feel-good/look-good phenomenon isn't just about waxing. With [actor] George Clooney, aka the 'king of grown-up grooming', as a style hero, today's urban man is happily discovering the relaxing delights of manicures and pedicures, deep-cleansing facials, stress-busting cranial massages and—thank heavens—trimming those tufty eyebrows and hairy ears. There's even a marked increase in high-tech treatments like microdermabrasion and Botox among high-flyers and those in the public eye—though judging by [Prime Minister] Tony Blair's ever-deepening wrinkles, the rumours of his Botox treatments are untrue. Those too reticent to make the first move into the world of pampering that we women take for granted are often prodded into action by being bought a gift voucher.

Thereafter it seems they are hooked, and male-only salons such as Duke & Co. and the newly launched Nickel are part of a burgeoning business.

Back home in the bathroom, the alpha male has brushed up on his technique. He now knows that dipping into his partner's pot of Crème de la Mer isn't going to work. Male skin is 22 per cent thicker than women's, has a higher acid pH, more sebum and a tendency to dehydrate more quickly. This means that the formula used to create a male product really does have to be different. Annoyingly for us girls, men's skin also ages more slowly. For both sexes, however, skin care rules are the same: 'keep it clean, keep it exfoliated and keep it moisturised'. With Christmas shopping in mind, there is a bewildering arsenal of creams, serums, oils and unguents specifically for men. Given it's party time, Christmas spirit [alcohol] has probably hit the liver hard—which in turn dulls the skin. Milk thistle tablets should do the trick for the former, while Clarins Men Fatigue Fighter (promoted as being great for tired and hungover skin) should keep your face in great shape.

VIEWPOINT 2

Skin Lightening Is Insulting to Black People

Mica Paris

Television presenter Mica Paris is concerned about an advertising campaign in London's Daily Mail, *where African American singer Beyoncé Knowles appeared with lighter skin and straighter hair than she normally does. Paris believes that advertisers want a popular black celebrity to represent them, but fear that white people won't buy their products if her skin and hair appear too dark. She hopes that Beyoncé will fight back and demand to be represented in advertising in her true color.*

As you read, consider the following questions:

1. What other women does Paris say have had their color misrepresented in advertising?
2. What does the author say is the effect of this type of advertising on young black girls?
3. What did the Italian *Vogue* magazine do with black models? Was it successful?

The latest ad campaign from L'Oréal has caused a huge stir by featuring a picture of singer Beyoncé Knowles looking much lighter-skinned than usual, her hair strawberry blonde. So has the picture been doctored to make her more attractive

Mica Paris, "Beyond the Pale; Beyoncé Is the Latest Star to Look Mysteriously Lighter in a Beauty Ad," *Daily Mail*, August 14, 2008, p. 57.

to white consumers? L'Oréal denies lightening Beyoncé's skin tone, but she's not the first black or ethnic model to appear in a makeup advert [advertisement] looking bleached out. Here, TV presenter Mica Paris, 39, argues that the campaign is a betrayal of black women.

When I picked up the *Daily Mail* and saw the two faces of Beyoncé staring back at me, I was angry and upset.

In one picture, she looked as she does in the flesh—black, beautiful and proud. But in the second—a bizarre and unreal image issued by L'Oréal to advertise their products—this black icon has been bleached out to the point where it looks like they are trying to turn her white.

It wasn't even a case of Beyoncé's skin looking paler and washed out.

Her hair had also been straightened with not a wave in sight, as if this was just one more step towards making her look Caucasian white instead of African American.

This is no trick of the light. It's a deliberate attempt to lighten a black person in the hope of widening her appeal—it's not the only example.

They want 'hip' Beyoncé to endorse their products, as she brings a young and 'with-it' feel, but they don't want to alienate the white big spenders. The answer? Have it both ways—a 'bleached' black face.

Diana Ross looks much paler than normal in a MAC cosmetics ad, while the Hispanic Eva Longoria is anaemic [anemic] in a poster for L'Oréal hair products.

What is truly disturbing about the image of Beyoncé is that L'Oréal has taken one of the most talented and beautiful black women in the world, and, in my view, has deliberately lightened her colour and hair in order to sell a beauty product.

This has to be the ultimate insult to every black woman out there—Beyoncé included. It is suggesting that in order to be beautiful and appealing, she needs to be white.

Advertisers Panic About Using Black Models

I've met Beyoncé, and I can't imagine she would be happy with what they have done. But advertisers panic about using black models—it scares them. I am convinced that they believe a black face on a product will alienate white people, and result in a drop in sales.

I can't believe this would be the case in today's multicultural society—but the middle-class, white, middle-aged managers who make these decisions probably come from an entirely different era.

They want 'hip' Beyoncé to endorse their products, as she brings a young and 'with-it' feel, but they don't want to alienate the white big spenders. The answer? Have it both ways—a 'bleached' black face.

By doing this, they believe they are appealing to the widest audience.

Airbrushing, of course, is perfectly normal. I've been airbrushed myself, but never have my very dark skin or straight nose been altered. Nor would I ever allow it to be.

It is hard to make your way as a bright, beautiful and independent black woman in today's society.

Beyoncé has fought so hard to get where she has, but the message beaming out from her lightened face, perfectly straight hair and altered image is hugely disturbing.

Altering a Black Image Takes Away Role Models from Young Black Girls

What does it say to young black girls? Hide the fact that you are black? Your skin colour is something to be ashamed of? Beyoncé's lightened image screams the message that you can't stand up and be proud to be black.

Skin Lightening Is Big Business Across Asia

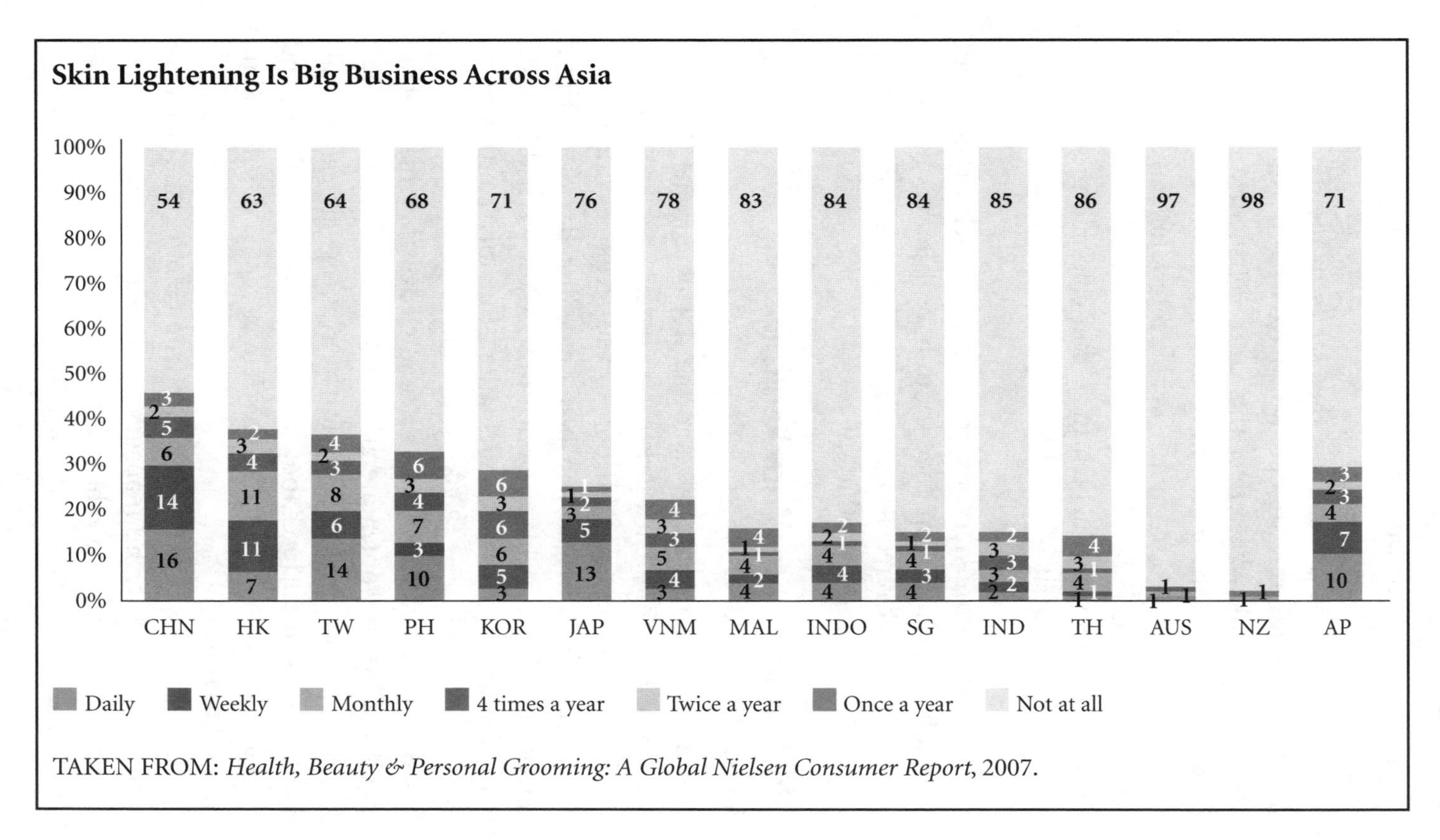

TAKEN FROM: *Health, Beauty & Personal Grooming: A Global Nielsen Consumer Report*, 2007.

Yet this is why we are having so much trouble on the streets today.

Young black kids can't see themselves in the media. They are desperate for role models who have become successful. I shudder to think what effect this computer-generated image of Beyoncé might have on young female fans out there.

Decades ago, black women in the entertainment industry, such as the singer Josephine Baker, were forced to use lemon juice in an attempt to lighten their skin colour. I thought this was barbaric, but it is no different to what has happened to Beyoncé.

Advertisers are nervous about using black models, but with a bit of 'Photoshop' they try to have it both ways.

In the UK [United Kingdom], it is rare to see black models used to promote products.

Black Images Are More Realistic Outside the UK

When I travel through Italy and the rest of Europe, there are images of beautiful black girls everywhere.

But advertisers should look to the recent example from the Italian *Vogue* magazine, where one editor dared to print a special edition using black models only. Many warned it would have disastrous results on circulation. But this 'controversial' issue, in July this year [2008], sold out.

But when will advertisers acknowledge that black, Hispanic and Asian women are also consumers.

Beyoncé is a great signing for L'Oréal, she appeals to millions of fans of all races, but to be afraid of what she is, and to alter that to make her commercially acceptable is degrading and infuriating.

If Beyoncé wants to show her true colours, she needs to fight back. And if she manages to change the way industry chiefs view darker skin, then she will prove her true worth as a black icon.

VIEWPOINT 3

Some Muslims Break with Tradition and Obtain Cosmetic Surgery

Ruth Nasrullah

Some Muslims say that plastic surgery is forbidden, while others point to reasons why they believe it is acceptable. In the following viewpoint, Ruth Nasrullah, a journalist who often writes about Muslim issues, outlines some of the religious questions Muslims have to consider when deciding whether or not to have plastic surgery.

As you read, consider the following questions:

1. How does Nasrullah explain the difference between cosmetic and reconstructive surgery?
2. What does the author say is the consensus of Islamic religious leaders about plastic surgery?
3. How does Mahjabeen Hassan's opinion differ from that of these religious leaders?

Wrinkles, sagging skin and cellulite. One or all are unavoidable if you're a woman. Genetics and lifestyle can minimize them, but there are no guaranteed ways to diminish the signs of aging and the effects of weight gain. Nevertheless, many women give it a try with a very popular option—through cosmetic surgery.

Ruth Nasrullah, "Skin Deep," *Azizah*, vol. 4, no. 3, November 2006, pp. 43–46. Reproduced by permission from Azizah Magazine.

Cosmetic procedures of all types are becoming increasingly common. A member survey by the American Society of Plastic Surgeons shows that between 2000 and 2005 there was a 150 percent increase in the number of cosmetic procedures performed—and an astounding 775 percent increase since 1992. In 2005, 10.2 million cosmetic procedures were performed, including 1.8 million surgical and 8.4 million "minimally invasive" procedures, such as Botox injections and laser hair removal.

There are no statistics on how many of these patients are Muslim women. In a society where even modest clothing is at odds with the culture at large, the issues surrounding cosmetic procedures may be thornier for Muslims than for other women.

Plastic Surgery Can Be Reconstructive or Cosmetic

Before considering those issues, let's understand the basics. Plastic surgery encompasses two types of procedures—cosmetic and reconstructive. Reconstructive procedures improve both function and appearance of deformities, whether caused by disease or accident. Such procedures may include correction of congenital deformities like cleft palates, or reconstruction from burns or other injuries, as well as breast reconstruction after a mastectomy. Insurance companies pay for reconstructive procedures far more easily than cosmetic procedures.

Cosmetic surgery involves changing normally functioning body structures in order to improve appearance. These procedures range from one-time, low-risk treatments like superficial chemical peels or Botox injections to serious surgery requiring general anesthesia and prolonged recovery time. Common cosmetic procedures such as abdominoplasty (tummy tuck) and breast enlargement may take several hours to complete and from weeks to months for full recovery. These procedures require an investment in time and money—with the money investment often substantial because most health insurance plans don't cover cosmetic surgery. The national average cost of a tummy tuck is in the neighborhood of $4,500, a nose job is around $3,301 and a face-lift can be $5,000.

Many major surgeries such as tummy tucks or breast lifts leave extensive scars, restrict activities and may not show final results for months. Some procedures ultimately require revision. The outcomes aren't certain, either immediately after surgery or long term. No procedure guarantees permanence and nothing is risk-free.

Muslim Women Have to Consider Religious Issues

In addition to the risks and costs, Muslim women considering plastic surgery may have religious reservations and seek advice from an Islamic perspective. The consensus of Islamic religious leaders is that surgery done solely for aesthetic reasons is not permissible in Islam. The verse often cited as evidence is verse 119 of Surah An-Nisa': "I will mislead them, and I will create in them false desires; I will order them to slit the ears of cattle, and to deface the fair nature created by God. Whoever, forsaking God, takes Satan for a friend, has of a surety suffered a loss that is manifest."

Sheikh Zoubir Bouchikhi, imam of the Islamic Society of Greater Houston, asserts that there are only two situations in which plastic surgery is permissible in Islam—to save a life or to correct a defect. He explains that surgery intended solely to beautify is a way of denying that Allah created us in a perfect form. "That is a form of rebellion against God Almighty, telling Him that You did not create me nice. You should have created me right," declares the sheikh.

Two hadith [records of the sayings of Muhammad] are frequently quoted to inform those seeking guidance on the topic. One states Abdullah said, "Allah's curse is on those women who practice tattooing and get themselves tattooed, and those who remove hair from their faces, and those who make space between their teeth artificially to beautify themselves. They change the nature and features created by Allah. Allah's Messenger cursed such women." Although scholars don't uniformly agree on what may be banned based on this hadith, it is often presented as evidence.

Other scholars refer to the occasion when the Prophet, peace be on him, allowed a man whose nose had been damaged in battle, to replace it with one made of gold. They offer this as justification for cosmetic surgery to correct a defect.

Muslim Surgeons Have to Consider What Is Appropriate

The line between defect and glamour is not always clear. Dr. Yusuf Al-Qaradawi noted on IslamOnline.net that cosmetic surgery for a deformity is allowable if someone "has an unusual physical defect, which attracts the attention of others to the point of inflicting on him physical and psychological pain every time he meets people."

The final decision lies in the hands of the Muslim patient and practitioner. Dr. Hiyad Al-Husaini, a Muslim plastic surgeon in New York City, acknowledges that it's not always an easy call. "I don't think there are any clear-cut rulings, especially regarding where the line is between reconstructive and cosmetic," she relates. "If, say, there's a functional problem with the nose, sometimes the cosmetic issue will improve both the look and the function. But many other cases just fall in the gray zone." Although she doesn't have many Muslim patients, if any should ask her about the propriety of surgery, she replies that she's not the authority to ask, nor being a religious authority.

Dr. Mahjabeen Hassan, a Muslim plastic surgeon with a practice in Westchester County, New York, is familiar with the verse in Surah An-Nisa' about not changing the body, but she believes that Allah gave us sufficient "wisdom and intellect" to discern what constitutes appropriate change. "Am I competing

Jewish Objections to Plastic Surgery

The first potential practical objection to plastic surgery is the Torah obligation to guard health which might limit the surgical risks that one may accept as part of plastic surgery. In addition to the hazards associated with the surgery itself, anesthesia, particularly general anesthesia, presents a very small but real risk of death or incapacitation.

Beyond the blanket obligation to guard health, there is the particular prohibition of self-mutilation. Just as one may not injure someone else, one may not cause injury to oneself. The prohibition of injuring someone else is called *chavala* and is derived directly from the biblical verse that warns the court not to give a convicted criminal more lashes than legally mandated. . . .

The Talmud [a central text of Judaism] discusses whether this prohibition applies to harming oneself, concluding that "one who injures himself even though it is forbidden, pays no damages. But if someone else injures him, they pay damages." . . . We are only barred from causing unnecessary injury to ourselves. The key question is what is considered necessary.

Risk and harming oneself are not the only issues. There are also philosophical considerations. Do we assert that God, as the ultimate craftsman and molder of human beings, makes each person exactly as they should be and that our "remodeling" of ourselves is an affront to His judgment? That is, does the divine mandate to heal and obligation to seek medical treatment extend to plastic surgery?

Daniel Eisenberg,
"Judaism and Cosmetic Surgery,"
Aish.com, May 20, 2006. www.aish.com

with God? No, not at all," explains Dr. Hassan. She considers herself fortunate to be able to help Muslim women, and all women for that matter, especially in cases of reconstructive surgery.

She acknowledges that humility must, accompany the sense of satisfaction. "When I see a patient I have helped, all I can do is bow my head before my Creator," she reflects.

Najwa [name has been changed], one of her patients, has had Botox injections and sees nothing wrong with taking such a step to improve her appearance. She cites Prophet Muhammad's high standard for good grooming and dress as a model for maintaining a good appearance. She thinks it's likely that Muslim women forego cosmetic procedures not for religious reasons, but because of other issues such as discouragement by their husbands. Her own husband, she says, told her she looks fine. But she doesn't like the wrinkles around her eyes, and since she had never heard that it was haram [forbidden], she says, "I went for it!"

In contrast, Zahrah [name has been changed] was quite hesitant about having plastic surgery. Seven years ago, she was feeling very unappealing to her husband who seemed to be loosing interest in her. Without informing him, she elected to have a face-lift, liposuction and a tummy truck. "It was a time in my life when I was feeling old and unattractive to my husband," she recounts. "I had serious reservations. If you're not to even pluck your eyebrows, what about plastic surgery? But I was told there was a hadith of Aishah's that says women should do whatever they can to be attractive to their husbands. That's how I rationalized the surgery."

Muslims Have to Consider Reasons for Plastic Surgery

Do advertising and society influence Muslim women's choices and inclinations regarding plastic surgery? Sheikh Bouchikhi's view is that beauty is relative and a woman who pursues surgical means to achieve attractiveness is following her own nafs [self] and the whispering of the shaitan [devil].

Some cases really push the envelope. A procedure that has recently gained media and medical attention is hymenoplasty, the surgical repair of the hymen, the membrane covering the entrance to the vagina. This operation effectively restores a woman to a "virginal" state. It has been reported in American and British medical journals that women who come from countries where virginity is prized and premarital sex is punished—many of whom are Muslim—have resorted to hymenoplasty in the US [United States] and returned home without the evidence of illicit intercourse.

For Muslim women, [plastic surgery] also requires consideration of the range of Islamic viewpoints in order to feel comfortable that surgery is necessary from a medical, lifestyle, and most of all, a spiritual standpoint.

Another cosmetic trend growing worldwide is the surgical altering of ethnic features. One striking example is the number of Asians increasingly electing to have surgery to make their eyes appear more "Western." Eyes are not the only offending body parts. According to the *Tehran Times*, the Islamic Republic of Iran is becoming famous as "the nose job capital of the world" as Iranians—both women and men are following a remarkable craze for facial surgery. Last year [2005], CBS reported that while liposuction is the most popular cosmetic procedure in the US, in Iran it is nose jobs.

A smaller nose, wider eyes or a tighter face do not always bring satisfaction; Zahrah is doubtful she would ever submit to the cosmetic scalpel again. "I didn't feel much better afterwards. It would be different if I was into that type of thing, but I didn't do it for myself. I did it for my husband and to save my marriage," she relates.

When Zahrah returned from her extended vacation, her husband failed to notice her surgical rejuvenation. Nevertheless, the marriage remained intact and thrived.

What cosmetic surgery boils down to is an intentional and selective choice to change one's appearance. To do so isn't—and shouldn't be, for the sake of certainty—an easy decision. It involves, to varying extents, risk, money, and sacrifice. For Muslim women, it also requires consideration of the range of Islamic viewpoints in order to feel comfortable that surgery is necessary from a medical, lifestyle, and most of all, spiritual standpoint.

Viewpoint 4

Ethiopian Tribes Practice Body Painting

Hans Silvester

In an area of Ethiopia called the Omo Valley, native tribes still carry on their lives with little influence from Western culture. Two of these tribes, the Surma and the Mursi, wear almost no clothing, but instead paint their bodies with natural pigments and decorate them with items such as skins, leaves, grass, and flowers. Photographer Hans Silvester has visited and photographed these tribes, and in the following viewpoint, he writes about what he has seen.

As you read, consider the following questions:

1. Besides paint, what are some natural items that the villagers use to decorate their bodies?
2. From where do the pigments for paints come?
3. What does the author say happened because there are no mirrors available?

An arena of incessant tribal and guerrilla warfare, and a hotbed for the arms and ivory trades, the Omo Valley [in Ethiopia] nevertheless plays host—when the Kalashnikovs [rifles] fall silent—to some astonishing events of a much more peaceful nature. Among the fifteen tribes that have lived in

Hans Silvester, *Natural Fashion: Tribal Decoration from Africa*, translated by David H. Wilson, London, UK: Thames & Hudson, 2008.

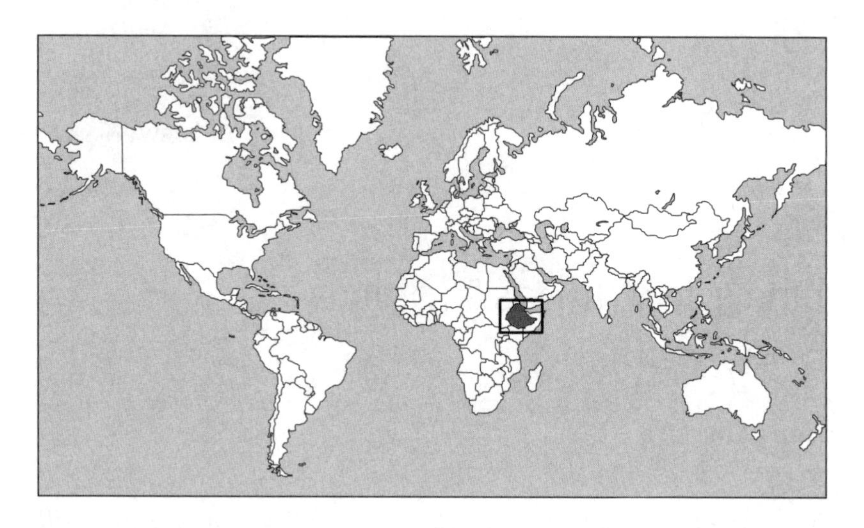

this Rift region since time immemorial, the Surma and the Mursi, two tribes that get on well together, share a taste for body painting and extravagant decorations borrowed from nature. The former is done mainly with materials from the plant world, whereas the latter predominantly comprises products of the hunt—all kinds of trophies, including buffalo horns, warthog tusks, monkey skins and more.

These displays often have a practical origin, such as protection against the sun. Thus when women walk from one village to another, they frequently carry a branch to provide themselves with some shade. Afterwards, they paint, decorate and embellish themselves with ingredients drawn from the vast store cupboard of Mother Nature. Renewed every day, these wonderfully inventive changes of appearance form a parade of African fashion that is as rich as it is ephemeral. A little lump of clay stuck on top of the head and pierced with feathers becomes a masterpiece of the milliner's art. Zebu skin sheathing the shins is transformed into an original pair of bush leggings. Snail shells strung on plant fibre make a superb necklace. Shells, nuts, gourds, flowers, woven grass are all used for decoration. A scattering of non-natural items—rifle cartridges, the tops of ballpoint pens, pieces of Italian glass jewelry—sometimes supplement these ornaments, as a reminder that Western civilization, even in the deepest depths of Africa, is never far away. As for copper bracelets, the last word in luxury, these come from Uganda and are acquired for the price of so many goats.

Generally naked—only the women wear a tiny G-string—the bodies are smooth and supple, providing an extraordinary sculptural surface that is ideal for these works of art. Flesh becomes a raw material on which decorative fantasies can be played out. Heads are almost completely shaven, and this creates a minimalistic effect, with just a few discreet elements of decoration: a tiny circle, triangle or tuft—each motif representing a sign specific to one family, much like our own coats of arms. For the most part, the Surma and Mursi use Indian-made razor blades to shape their geometric hairstyles. Failing these, they make do with leaf springs from Land Rovers which they take to pieces and sharpen.

The earlobes of boys as well as girls are usually pierced, and the holes are gradually enlarged with slivers of wood, each one bigger than the last—technique similar to that used by the womenfolk with their discs. These piercings hold various decorations, like fruits, snail shells, pieces of pottery and other trinkets. There is, however, nothing obligatory in this practice, and some people prefer to leave their ears intact. Families are free to do what they want, and the only compulsory mark comes later and applies to girls of marriageable age. When they reach about twenty, they have to undergo an incision of the lower lip, into which is inserted a 'disc'—a tradition which has unfortunately persisted right through to the present. It is an extremely brutal custom, but is all the more entrenched because of the fact that a girl bearing this token will earn a great deal more for her father, since her bridal price may even double—fifty cows instead of the twenty or twenty-five normally paid by the prospective husband.

Body Painting Is Common Throughout the World

Paint is one of the most common ways to accentuate the face and body. The Wodaabe, a subgroup of the Fulani, travel with their camels and cattle in small bands throughout Niger, northern Nigeria, and northeast Cameroon. During the rainy season, when the land can sustain large herds, families come together to participate in the Gerewol festival. It is during this festival that young male Wodaabe herders take part in the *yaake* dance. They spend many hours preparing their face paint and costumes to conform to the Wodaabe ideal of beauty. Their face is typically painted yellow with a vertical stripe down the nose and chin, partitioning the face into two halves and visually lengthening the face. Dancers also use turbans topped with ostrich feathers and long strings of beads at the sides of their faces and tunics to create height. White circles are cast on the cheeks, forehead, and chin. Performers also paint black lines around their eyes and lips. . . .

The peoples of the Nuba Mountains in Sudan use paint and hair dressing to designate their life cycle stage. A newborn baby is anointed with red or yellow ochre to be initiated into this world. When a man is in his prime, patterning the body with color is essential to looking attractive. . . . In the early twenty-first century, the Sudanese government discourages the displaying of the unclothed, painted body. However, the vast dissemination of this practice in the Western world through popular photographs has motivated some Nuba men to paint for the financial incentive of tourism.

Peri M. Klemm, "Cosmetics and Body Painting," New Encyclopedia of Africa. *Eds. John Middleton and Joseph C. Miller. Detroit, MI: Thomson/Gale, 2008.*

The Body Is a Canvas to Be Decorated

This decorative focus on the body, and its preeminence over the spatial environment and the surrounding world of objects, is strongly connected with nomadic lifestyles. The body is seen almost as a piece of territory, with skin and flesh replacing the stone, ceramics and textiles typical of other cultures. Nomads always have the ability to leave everything behind and travel. Except for their livestock—the only wealth they own—their possessions are limited to what they can carry on their backs or shoulders. The inventory is short: a few plain pots of clay, some gourds, things to eat and drink, skins to lay out on the ground, and weapons—knives for the women and children, Kalashnikovs for the men. Their homes are very simple and made exclusively of plant materials. They do not use mud or clay, but only branches. The one item that is sometimes ornate is the headrest, which old people use and which also serves as a stool. Shaped from a piece of white wood, it is decorated with a sort of rudimentary pokerwork: Cow dung is smeared on it to form different motifs, lines or dots. Live embers are then applied and the uncovered surfaces of the wood blacken, while the rest retains the bright colour of the original.

It is right beside the river, the lifeline of the region, that these decorative arts are at their most expressive. At the peak of the dry season, during the weeks that precede the arrival of the rains, the weather in these latitudes becomes extremely heavy, with temperatures around 45° C [113° F]. The sky turns a whitish grey, almost leaden. At this time, much of village life takes place by the river, which is the only source of water for humans as well as animals. It is quite shallow, unlike the Omo, which is dangerous and infested with crocodiles, not to mention various species of lizard that sometimes haunt its little tributaries. People come to draw water, or bring their cattle to drink; they also fish there in somewhat primitive fashion for catfish, to supplement their stocks of grain, sorghum and maize, which dwindle fast at this time of year. And they bathe there too, looking to escape from the intense heat. Children, youths and adults all come together where the water has dug out shallow coves, never more than two metres [about 6.5 feet] in depth, for them to swim in.

The final effect, while not sophisticated, is by no means crude. There is a fascinating dimension of mystery here that is almost magical.

In this region of East Africa, the savannah landscape presents a picture of large, scattered trees and bushes, and tall dry grasses. In contrast, the vegetation near the water is almost lush—papyrus, flowers, and wild fruit trees. This luxuriance is like an incitement to self-expression, to putting on a show. Within easy reach is a multitude of plants, each one an invitation to indulge in all kinds of imaginative decoration. A tuft of grass serves as a hat, and banana leaves, woven tendrils or flowers are knotted together like a scarf or neckerchief. For Westerners, any such activity might demand great intellectual effort—which branch, what colour, how and where should they be arranged?—and the whole process could seem laborious, but here the people make their choices spontaneously but firmly, and with a particular instinct for what will work. They do not spend any time thinking about it. They live so close to nature that they also act naturally, and at quite astonishing speed. They take a branch, strip it, adroitly turn it into a string, and weave that into a crown or some other form, to be finished off with a shell as its centrepiece.

The final effect, while not sophisticated, is by no means crude. There is a fascinating dimension of mystery here that is almost magical. Anyone who has observed these people for any length of time will see that they are remarkably talented: They can take any material from the plant world—leaf, stem, flower, grass, root—and instantly transform it into an accessory that has come straight from a fantasy or fairy tale, without the slightest tinge of absurdity. This skill is an integral feature of those human societies that live in symbiosis with nature. For them, she provides an infinite wardrobe—the most amazing accessory shop you can imagine.

Mother Nature Provides an Array of Colours

Attractive though they are, these plant decorations might be nothing but somewhat extravagant accoutrements, were they not accompanied by body paintings which create a kind of decorative counterbalance. Done with the aid of natural pigments, these constitute the abstract element in this style of physical adornment.

The geological structure of the volcanic Rift Valley is quite remarkable. Some rock faces reveal strata of red, ochre, yellow, all shades of white, pure white and light grey. This mixture of pigments dating from aeons ago offers a vast palette of colours, with the single exception of blue. They are very concentrated and pure. A small piece of ochre crushed with a pebble will yield a quantity of pale colour when diluted with plenty of water, whereas just a few drops will create a darker shade. Green is obtained from a crumbly stone found on the riverbed; this must be broken and then crushed into a powder.

The richness and beauty of these pigments are seen at their brightest and best when combined with the individual colour and texture of the skin. This is linked to the reflection of light. Further to the south, very dark-skinned people—the Sudanese, Kenyans and Ugandans—absorb light, but the Omo tribes, native Ethiopians from the mountains, have a complexion that is redder, more copper-coloured. They do not consider themselves to be black, and they do not have negroid features. Their skin reflects the light very well, and so provides a wonderful background for the various pigments.

Having No Mirrors Provides Freedom

These body paintings are totally free, and yet they never repeat themselves, and there is no underlying system. Each one is extraordinarily fresh. The technique and the skill of body decoration, with its infinite variations, is learned at a very early age, with mothers painting their babies. But it is adolescents who devote themselves most avidly to this activity. Some of them are immensely talented. They have a highly original sense of colour and form, whereas others can be clumsy and need to start all over again. In the case of any second thoughts, a dive into the river will provide a fresh start, although the process cannot of course be reversed.

Most of the painting is done by hand. Cruder motifs are drawn very quickly with a finger, but details are executed with the aid of a piece of reed. This is split between two stones. One end serves as a sort of swab, and its splayed fibres can draw things like stars or birds' footprints. A sharpened piece is used to draw dots and spots.

The absence of mirrors—until recently, these were completely unknown to the tribes—may have contributed to the absolute freedom of this art. Without a mirror or even a natural equivalent (the silty water is always cloudy in the valley), the only way one can see oneself is through other people's reactions. Reflections, or narcissistic images in the mythical sense, do not exist. An image of oneself, if we can talk of such a thing, can therefore only be constructed through the eyes of others. And also, to a certain degree, through the lens of the camera. Might not this situation make people invent something crazy, something extreme, in order to create a reaction, whereas a mirror is merely a mirror? For this very reason, body painting is not done in isolation. For it to be effective, the presence of a second person is indispensable, at least as far as the face and back are concerned. But often you will find five or even ten people together by the water. Body painting is thus very much a team sport.

Body Painting Is an Art Form

Quite apart from the playful pleasures of the activity, the young painters are also very proud of their art. They are aware that they are doing something important, as is evident from their intense concentration. When they paint one another, their faces are very serious. One is reminded in certain respects of Japanese Noh theatre. This is marked by a complete absence of visible expression. But do not be misled—there is nothing clown-like about Mursi and Surma body painting, and there is no sense of dressing up either, as in the carnival tradition, in which people change their appearance or their role. What we have here is a skill and an art form that is an integral element of the culture. The very fact that a painting may be erased in the waters of the river if it does not fulfill the artist's intention, so that he or she can start all over again, confirms that there is a concept of failure or success, and it greatly enhances the value of a tradition that has been passed down from generation to generation. As a cultural manifestation, the act of painting and decorating oneself is of almost religious importance, despite its ephemeral and apparently anecdotal character.

Perhaps underlying it all is the spirit of the hunter, accustomed to the art of camouflage, or the warrior merging with nature as he confronts his enemy. Or perhaps it is simply an unconscious homage to Mother Earth.

Aside from the ashes with which shepherds sometimes smear their bodies to protect themselves against the sun and the flies that swarm round their flocks, it would be difficult to find any occasions, whether functional, festive or ritual, that specifically demand these body paintings, even among adults. People simply paint themselves for no particular reason and at no particular time.

The only hint of religious significance that I myself observed was the day after an incredible storm, which lit up the night with its bolts of lightning. After the deluge, which carried away tents and huts and trees, everyone in the village displayed three streaks of green on their foreheads, put on brusquely with three fingers. I was told by the interpreters that these signs were meant to appease the malevolent god of the storm and calm his destructive powers. But there does seem to be a strong link between the paintings and the deities, although the tribes themselves have very little to say about such questions and, in this particular case, very little to show—just three simple lines. It is true to say, however, that coded practices of this kind greatly reduce freedom of expression.

If one really has to find a reference for this art form, it would have to be in its mimicry of nature and of animals. One man might paint his own face in a manner clearly inspired by that of a monkey; someone else will colour his torso like an animal skin; another will make his legs look like the hanging tree roots of plants such as mangroves. Each artist reproduces the things he has seen through his close proximity to nature. Perhaps underlying it all is the spirit of the hunter, accustomed to the art of camouflage, or the warrior merging with nature as he confronts his enemy. Or perhaps it is simply an unconscious homage to Mother Earth.

Periodical Bibliography

The following articles have been selected to supplement the diverse views presented in this chapter.

Julie Beun-Chown	"From Guyliner to Man-scara: More Guys Are Wearing Makeup—and Not Just Rock Stars," *Ottawa Citizen* (Canada), June 30, 2009.
Christopher A.D. Charles	"Skin Bleaching, Self-Hate, and Black Identity in Jamaica," *Journal of Black Studies*, vol. 33, no. 6, 2003.
Sharon Guynup	"Scarification: Ancient Body Art Leaving New Marks," *National Geographic*, July 28, 2004.
Timothy A. Judge, Charlice Hurst, and Lauren S. Simon	"Does It Pay to Be Smart, Attractive, or Confident (or All Three)? Relationships Among General Mental Ability, Physical Attractiveness, Core Self-Evaluations, and Income," *Journal of Applied Psychology*, vol. 94, no. 3, 2009.
Peri M. Klemm	"Oromo Fashion: Three Contemporary Body Art Practices Among Afran Qallo Women," *Africa Arts*, Spring 2009.
Anthony Layng	"Color Counts," *USA Today* (Society for the Advancement of Education), March 2006.
Ibram Rogers	"More Ghanaians Equate Beauty with Looking White," *Diverse: Issues in Higher Education*, June 19, 2006.
C.M. Schorzman et al.	"Body Art: Attitudes and Practices Regarding Body Piercing Among Urban Undergraduates," *Journal of the American Osteopathic Association*, October 2007.
Stacie Stukin	"Youth in a Jar? Probably Not, but We Buy It Anyway," *Los Angeles Times*, July 13, 2009.

Chapter 4

Ethnic and Religious Dress

VIEWPOINT 1

Ethnic Dress and Modern Fashion Often Have a Complex Relationship

Margaret Maynard

Margaret Maynard is a fashion researcher at the University of Queensland, Australia. In the following viewpoint, she discusses the relationship between local ethnic dress and global fashion. Maynard talks about ways that global fashion design borrows from ethnic styles and the ways in which ethnic dress is sometimes combined with Western fashions.

As you read, consider the following questions:

1. Give two examples of clothing that Maynard describes as illustrating bicultural identity.
2. What does the author say journalists mean by "ethnic chic"?
3. How do women in Bouaké, West Africa, combine ethnic and Western clothing?

The uptake of Western dress among non-European cultures, with their own dress traditions, has been both selective and inconsistent. In some places, thoroughgoing adoption of European dress has taken place only since about the 1970s. In China for example, *shizhuang* or fashion, as a sign of

Margaret Maynard, *Dress and Globalisation*, Manchester, United Kingdom: Manchester University Press, 2004, pp. 76–86.

growing links to the international world, emerged only in the mid-1980s. Western clothing continues to be combined in some places with traditional dress, or partially adopted with respect to gender and age, or for particular occasions. In many cultures, or subgroups, global clothing is regarded as a sign of progress, as opposed to a clinging on to tradition. Whilst its attraction has been considerable, consumer preferences can sometimes be formally countered by nationalist desires to re-invent traditional dress, or by a self-conscious, often deliberate choice to retain ethnic attire. In nationalist Zaire, under the rule of Mobutu Sese Seko, an 'authenticity' code was enforced that prevented men from wearing coats and ties, and women from wearing jeans. Although not based on national traditions, men in Zaire were required to wear a version of the Mao suit called *abaco* with a cravat and not a tie to express national identity. In 1997 President Laurent-Désiré Kabila, on coming to power in the new Democratic Republic of the Congo, put similar prohibitions in place.

Women Have Been Slower to Westernize Dress than Men

The uptake of Western clothing in the less-developed world has varied most obviously according to gender, although in places like Mauritania it may be only children who wear Western-style attire. Even so, whilst women have been on the whole slower to modernise, they are now widely accepting Western dress all over the world, either partially or in its entirety. In her account of Indian dress, published in the mid-1990s, [anthropologist Emma] Tarlo found married women, other than a small, educated urban elite, continued to wear Indian dress, where men did not. This having been said, fashionable urban women might carry a mixture of clothes in their wardrobe, from the classical Indian sari [also saree], to hybrid clothes like the *shalwar kamiza* (tunic and trousers), and chic Western clothes and leisure wear like jeans. Even Indian village women, like the *Bharwads* (pastoral people), are slowly modernising, still dressing in traditional clothing of *kapdu* (upper garment) and *jimi* (waist cloth), but made in cheaper and thinner artificial fabrics such as machine woven polyester. So the penetration of Western-style clothing is evident if only in part, and, as has been shown, traditional dress itself undergoes modifications and changes of fashion. Interestingly the fascination for Western dress can sometimes be less an emulation of the values of the US [United States], than a deliberate decision made by consumers for culturally specific and internal reasons. Research among Bedouin women in Egypt's Western Desert shows they continue to wear traditional dress. Yet they express resistance to the older generation and the power structure of their own culture, by a subtle westernising of veil fabrics and the use of cosmetics.

In all cultures, wearing dress that is not your own is undertaken for specific reasons and occasions, and at times can be assumed almost like a provisional or performance costume. Young village men in Egypt who travel to Cairo, for instance, sometimes take on informal Western dress. They also have their hair cut short, in order to feel greater security and to pass in the city as someone connected to the power structure of the state. This is not upward mobility as such, but a calculated decision to take on the dress of another culture and class for a certain period of time, and thus partake of the benefits of that class. In Mexico, villagers take on a *mestizo* appearance when visiting towns and large markets. But according to [Chloe] Sayer [an expert on arts and crafts of Mexico], writing in the 1980s, traditional dress of Mazahua communities could merely be covered over on such trips. In an interesting assumption of bicultural identity or provisional identity, Western trousers were worn over *calzones* (drawers) and store-bought shirts over customary embroidered ones. Yet, as we have seen in Mauritania the reverse can happen, with store-bought clothing worn beneath customary attire. There are other examples of bicultural dressing. Tarlo cites a case of a *Rabari* student who changed each day into college clothes of [a] shirt and trousers at a friend's house, returning in the evening to change back into *deshi* (indigenous dress) for the sake of his wife who despised him in European-style clothes.

The relationship between modern dress and customary or 'ethnic' clothing is an intricate weave of habit, defiance, social pressure and taboos, political entanglements and posturing, perhaps too intricate to ever untie completely.

In the Arab world and within the Arab diaspora since the 1970s, attitudes toward Western dress have varied widely. Many women have signaled resistance to Western dress and materialism by adopting modern versions of traditional head-scarves, or in some instances the full *hijab* [a head scarf or modest dress worn by Muslim women]. Yet in Saudi Arabia there is a quite different response. There ethnicity in dress has become less and less evident. Elite women pride themselves on acquiring luxurious and specially designed Gulf-style couture clothing and jewellery as a particular way of signalling status. So when educated and cosmopolitan women wear European rather than indigenous dress, it is not everyday clothing. In Egypt, for instance, this attire is Western dress at its most expensive and luxurious. This means a woman is willing to go to some considerable expense, and social discomfort, to avoid using the *hijab*, thereby deliberately aligning herself with a wealthy European class, rather than local indigenous culture. The wearing of Muslim dress is patently selective and case specific. In Egypt educated working women often wear a hybrid mix of long European-style maxi skirt with *hijab*, or a modest head covering, a *mu'adabah*, a cosmopolitan version of the head scarf. A further complication arises because the same woman is likely to wear completely customary clothing in her own neighbourhood or after hours. In Bouaké, West

Africa, women of the professional, urban elite wear mixtures of a tailored *boubous*, that is a half-length or full gown of Islamic origin, or a *complet trois pagnes* with high heel shoes and matching handbag. In addition Muslim women will add a head scarf to either outfit.

Modern and 'Ethnic' Dress Have a Complex Relationship

So the relationship between modern dress and customary or 'ethnic' clothing is an intricate weave of habit, defiance, social pressure and taboos, political entanglements and posturing, perhaps too intricate to ever untie completely. Superficially, the ostensibly uniform-like nature, and almost insidious attraction, of some global attire seems to draw nations together at the level of style. Yet it can often be the perception of 'sameness', rather than its actual consumption, that springs to mind in any assessment of worldwide dress. The belief in global uniformity is an exaggeration, obscuring the subtle instances of regional, caste and ethnic differences. Added to this, 'ethnic' dress of all types and varieties is worn alongside global clothing, sometimes even biculturally. Nepal is an interesting example of these complexities. As in other places, such as eastern Indonesia, the kind of dress one wears is an important way to signal one's state of 'development' and progressiveness, or alternatively one's 'old-fashioned' ways. In Nepal, women, like men, are increasingly wearing European dress, but there are still groups of women, identifying themselves with high-caste Hindus, who deliberately continue to wear saris. Hindu culture believes itself to be superior to others and officially encourages sari wearing to indicate association with their 'developed' culture, in this case development is associated with traditional rather than Western dress practices. At the same time, high-caste Hindu women in Nepal see themselves as more advanced than their counterparts in the North who wear *chubbas* (long cross-over tunics tied with a thick sash).

They regard these people as 'backward'. So all patterns of wearing are clearly inflected by minor local cultural perceptions of difference and evaluation, and these variations are meaningful to those who have inside knowledge of local dispositions and customs, where they may not be evident to others.

Western High Fashion Adopts 'Ethnic Flavors' as Exotic

Western high fashion has demonstrated for centuries an unceasing appetite for novel ideas based on the 'primitive' or the exotic. Designers today, like corporate raiders, source inspiration indiscriminately from distant cultures, usually with scant regard for original context. 'Ethnic' and 'national' styles, culled from one's own backyard or further afield, are a seemingly never diminishing gold mine of resources, a design pool available for all. The term 'ethnic chic' is sometimes used by journalists to describe the high fashionable habit of outsiders, that is those who adopt an ethnic 'look' without any concern for the actual dress traditions of a culture. Often only shorthand signs of chinoiserie [reflecting Chinese qualities] or Indian decoration are all that is needed to represent an indigenous culture. Particularly noteworthy is the lack of specificity in the common use of the term 'ethnic'. It frequently refers superficially to the appearance of dress that is vaguely village-like or peasant-like, having a rough, handmade, decorative quality. Aside from this general appropriation of the idea of ethnicity, Western designers also seamlessly incorporate into their fashions actual items of traditional dress, textiles and accessories like beads, shawls and earrings. These are displayed almost as collector's items or even as trophies. European and US fashion designers, as widely different as [Jean Paul] Gaultier, Ralph Lauren, [John] Galliano, and Shirin Guild, have been, and still are in their various ways, fascinated with ethnic or vernacular designs, with their distinctive qualities and aura of the 'genuine' or handcrafted. African, Indian, Asian, Mexican, South American, Iran, Central European folk designs have all been fair game for fashion designers.

Importantly we seldom hear what indigenous people feel about this form of appropriation, or about the ways in which 'native' dress, traditionally part of complex family systems, symbolisms and frameworks, is undermined by assimilation, commercialisation and fashion treasure hunters. Yet, one must bear in mind that catwalk interest in indigenous designs can have the reverse effect, stimulating and renewing interest in traditional textile practices and body decoration. An interesting case of exploitation is documented in Guatemala, a country that in its early history had hundreds of distinctive village costumes. Only vestiges of pre-Colombian dress were evident by the late twentieth century. In the 1990s Mayan village women still wore the traditional *huipil* upper garment, wrap-around *corte* skirt and woven belt, although both men and women wore mixtures of Mayan and Western-style clothes. Village men sometimes wore hybrid, even bicultural outfits, consisting of long pants made of woven Mayan fabric and topped with short overpants derived from ancient times. [Professor of Latin American Studies Barbara] Brodman uses changing Mayan dress practices to highlight the vulnerability of these native peoples, whose ancient traditions are gradually being undermined by imported interference. She cites a particular instance of exploitation on the part of the ruling Ladinos, who liked to bask in the reflected glory of Mayan heritage. At the annual Folklore Festival in Cobán, officials organised a parade of exquisite indigenous garments and textiles to sell to fashion designers' representatives and buyers from around the world. Beauty contestants in regional costumes, required by law to attend, were paraded before the largely foreign audience. This was a source of humiliation for villagers, but of no financial gain to them.

The interweavings between modern fashion and traditional dress are complex. Tarlo discusses some instances in the 1980s when Indian women chose to wear extravagant versions of Indian clothing as a form of 'ethnic chic', with little relationship to actual village dress or traditional clothing. This was part of a new commercialisation of fashion at the time. Tarlo raises questions about this apparent return to traditional Indianness in fashion, suggesting it is a form of masquerade or performance of identity, a tasteful ethnicity, rather than sympathy for local village people. This represents an idealised return to a certain aspect of the past, safeguarding the exclusivity of the wearers, who are, of course, not peasants. It also speaks to, and on behalf of, an international audience rather than a local one. It is also a status seeking practice according to Tarlo, so that the minority Indian elite can differentiate themselves from the mass of jeans- and sari-wearing middle classes. Quite lacking in social commitment they just play at style, stepping into the village, at the precise time that the majority of villagers are stepping out. She quotes the case in 1989 of a glamorous Delhi socialite of mixed background from a wealthy Lahore family who chose to 'go ethnic' and to wear the clothes of a low caste *Bungri* woman, while living an otherwise wealthy life.

Indian Fashion Designers Reinterpret Traditional Dress

At exactly this time Indian fashion designers in Britain began to set up highly successful firms, making garments based on traditional patterns and also importing garments designed in India. In fact an explosion of fashion houses started up in response to a growing middle class of educated professional Indian, and indeed British women, interested in designer clothes that reinterpreted traditional dress and celebrated the cultural roots of migrants. So culturally mobile Indian women as well as Western women were able to wear modifications of 'ethnic'

Indian dress produced by Indian designers. Khan [a researcher] argues that this was a practice that suited dual cultural systems, obviating the necessity for choice between East and West, suggesting there was, in the early 1990s, still no uniquely British-Asian fashion. This acceptance of dual fashion systems may appear to be a form of hedging one's bets, yet the political reality is that choice is usually only available to the well-to-do. The fact that no fully hybrid style had emerged by that time means the various circumstances and cultural rationale for choice of wear was different in each case. Clearly 'ethnic' dress has different resonances for different classes and also for Indian women in both India and Britain, compared to British women.

As part of the kind of cultural exchange identified above, the saree, a garment with a very ancient tradition and still worn by older Indian women, has been given a new lease of life in versions made of modern fabrics and colours. Sarees are made in every quality, from the everyday purchase at a sidewalk stall in London suburbs like Alperton or Southall, to more highly exclusive shops selling exquisite designer sarees. Older style sarees are also remodelled into new retro items for sale in places like Camden [London] market. The 'new' saree is sold as a fashion and promoted as an advantage for a modern Indian woman, as was Western dress previously. As Nag [a researcher] shows in her study of modern Bengali sarees, by the 1990s women were being enticed to buy the 'new' saree by advertising copy that paradoxically did so by using the nostalgic imagery of its past and traditional notions of femininity. But it is not just the case of redefining the saree, Western markets are saturated with unspecific Indian-style garments and accessories. Fashion designers continually experiment with new versions of the *shalwar* suit, a set of garments made up of trousers, tunic-like *kameez* and co-ordinated *dupatta* or stole. They are also fascinated with the richness of regional Indian dress, incorporating elements from Bhopali *kurtas* and Alighari *pyjamas* into new and partially modern styles.

The interweaving between traditional Indian dress and European fashion is matched by similar interchanges between Japanese and Chinese dress. Overwhelmingly westernised centres like Hong Kong are returning to their past by inventing modern high fashions and accessories that draw heavily on traditional garments, the *ma kwa* jacket and the *cheung sam* for instance. Interestingly in Hong Kong, especially around the takeover of sovereignty in 1997, the popularity of the latter two garments, revived as modern outfits in polyester not silk, sat well with an expanding consciousness of cultural identity. These garments were also worn in New York by non-Chinese people, sometimes with backpacks and athletic shoes. . . .

Western Designers Use Japanese Designs

Western designers have had a long-standing attraction to Japanese clothing and fabric designs. Traditional kimonos seem to embody supposedly timeless qualities, and have been drawn to the bodily design aesthetic they express. The Japanese themselves regard traditional kimonos, chiefly used on ceremonial occasions in modern times, as the most beautiful native dress in the world. Its fabrics express the Japanese aesthetic sensibility to the seasons and 'in its folds is layered the soul of Japan'. So in different ways, both cultures see symbolic and artistic qualities in the kimono, and for some it almost holds quasi-spiritual qualities. Japanese fashion designers like Issey Miyake and Rei Kawakubo since the 1970s have inspired Europe by producing garments that echoed their own national dress traditions. But interestingly, matching Western fascination with Japanese 'ethnicity', the Japanese have redefined the parameters of European haute couture by a turning back to their own native traditions and philosophies, although both Kawakubo and [Yohji] Yamamoto resist the label 'Japanese'.

In an ironic twist, Japanese consumers, drawn in their thousands to tourist venues in Australia, are deeply attracted to the products of cheerful Australian leisure wear designers like Ken Done, Mambo and Balarinji. Of these, Balarinji is the label that most readily complies with an Australian ethnicity, in that it trades on links with indigenous culture, making much of its collaborations between Australian and Aboriginal designers. Balarinji is more than a very successful tourist market provider. In 1992, with acute marketing perception, the company signed an agreement with the Japanese company, Nitto Boseki, to put their designs onto Japanese clothing and accessories. What is interesting is that they specifically rework their Aboriginal type colours in a brighter range for Japanese tastes. So, for the Japanese tourist in Australia, and those who shop at boutiques in Tokyo, brightly coloured and breezy Australian clothing signals a type of exotic colourfulness. This paradoxically represents a sort of reverse aesthetic to the traditions of subtlety in Asian design. . . .

Within new configurations that combine both tradition and modernity, clothing reveals that its design is constantly in a state of flux, and that it continues to convey important and differentially decoded messages about change within the global environment.

Much of the significance of what is labelled 'ethnic' dress by the West lies in the ways different stakeholders variously use and evaluate traditional or indigenous commodities. What we term 'ethnicity' in dress is clearly mutable. At any one time, clothing, hairstyles and body modifications, derived initially from non-Western cultures, mean certain things in terms of high fashion in the developed world, but something very different within popular culture, and to those who practice 'alternative' lifestyles. Cosmetic or body arts like Indian and African henna skin painting (*mehndi*) can simultaneously be a symbolic indigenous practice, a European fashion statement (especially popular around 1996), a mass marketed product (2000) but also an 'alternative' lifestyle accessory. Unquestionably customary 'ethnicity', expressed in dress, has been compromised and decontextualised by contact with the West, although the reverse may also be true, and global dress itself is subject to a high degree of variability. But within new configurations that combine both tradition and modernity, clothing reveals that its design is constantly in a state of flux, and that it continues to convey important and differentially decoded messages about change within the global environment.

VIEWPOINT 2

Indonesian Muslims Combine Traditional and Contemporary Fashion

Carla Jones

Carla Jones is an anthropologist who studies gender and class issues in Indonesia. In the following viewpoint, she discusses a form of dress called busana Muslim *or* Islami, *which combines fashionable features with traditional Muslim requirements for covering the body with a long, loose-fitting garment and head covering. She describes how* busana Muslim *is becoming popular in Indonesia with some women who want to dress fashionably while still respecting their Muslim heritage and beliefs.*

As you read, consider the following questions:

1. Why did a woman named Ibu Tia, who was interviewed by the author, say she chose to change from Western dress to *busana Muslim*?
2. Name three reasons that Jones says that Ibu Evi chooses to wear *busana Muslim* at least 30 percent of the time.
3. The author talks about a group of young Muslim women taking a course on instructional femininity. Why does she say these women choose to wear *busana Muslim*?

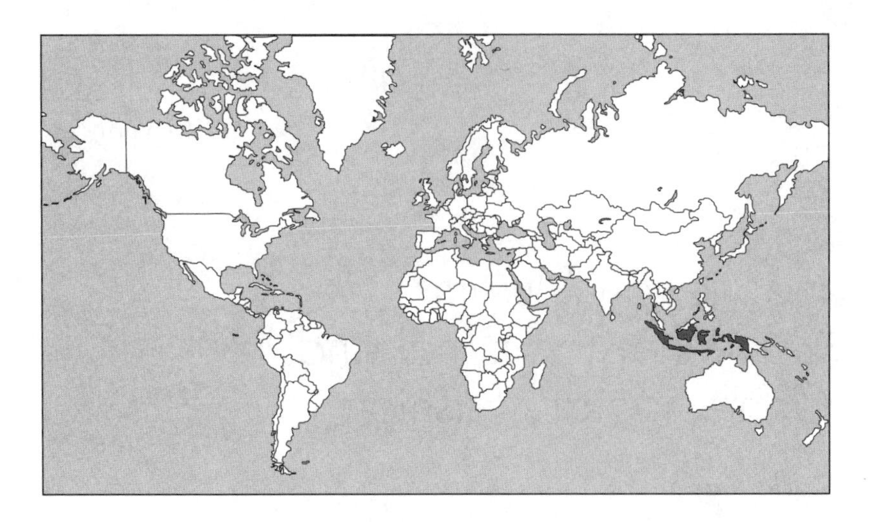

In the last decade in urban Indonesia, women's fashions have been influenced by explicitly Islamic forms of dress that are variously called *busana Muslim* or *Islami*. Versions of long-sleeved and floor-length garments, and loose or fitted head coverings, have become so common as to indicate a trendy transformation of a subgenre of dress and personal appearance that, until the early 1980s in Indonesia, was so unusual as to seem rare and foreign. This proliferation of Islamic dress, and associated Islamic material culture in urban Indonesia, is the result of an intersection of political, economic, and cultural changes. . . .

Deciding to Wear *Busana Muslim*

> Mbak Carla, you know, I really feel different in *busana Muslim*. I think I should wear it now, even though I am only 28 and I always thought I wouldn't wear it until I was much older, because it makes me behave differently. I want to go on the *hajj* [a Muslim pilgrimage to Mecca] someday, and I need to work on becoming closer to God before I can go, and when I wear *baju Muslim* I cannot forget God. . . . Besides, these clothes are more flattering on me since I have

> become a mother. And my husband is reminded that I am a good wife when he looks at me! He can't forget that I am moral.

Ibu Tia shared this with me on a hot afternoon in Yogyakarta in 1998 after I expressed surprise at seeing her twirling around her cramped living quarters in *busana Muslim* for the first time. In over a year of thrice-weekly conversations, I had had no idea that she was considering adopting *busana Muslim* and on that day we immediately fell into a conversation about whether the lace on her *kerudung* [a tailored veil] was too matronly and whether the shade of peach in her blouse was right for her skin tone. Tia's comments suggested that her adoption of Islamic dress, a change that ultimately was gradual and only completed over several months (in part because of the substantial expense entailed in a radical wardrobe change), was embedded in a web of influences, including interest in maintaining her husband's respect for her, her individual desire to become more devout, and concern about her changing figure. During our months of friendship, I had come to recognize the power Tia invested in some commodities in her life. Unbeknownst to her husband, she was quietly saving money in order to renovate their kitchen into the style modeled on television soap operas, because she admired the kind of ideal family dynamic portrayed on those shows. In addition, she was delighted that her infant son's favorite toy was a plastic cell phone, as she hoped that it would instill in him an interest in activities that would later benefit him as a businessman. In each of these examples, objects had the potential to create a different social world. Yet Tia also acknowledged that the potential was always only partial, and that in order for each to become realized, she would have to invest effort and intention for them to come to fruition. She insisted that her change of dress styles was primarily motivated by her desire to perfect her individual relationship with God, which was something that no one else could assess or know, and that improving her elationship with God would benefit all those around her, especially her son. She had increased her private Koranic study well before her change in wardrobe; yet found that her wardrobe change had itself motivated further study.

Busana Muslim Became a Stylish Choice

By the late 1990s and the end of the [Indonesian president] Soeharto regime, the landscape of Islamic fashions had altered significantly from its youth-associated and critical roots of the 1980s. Rather than seeming a biting social critique, or feeling foreign, *busana Muslim* had come to feel more like an unsurprising consumer choice among an array of dress styles for young women, Islamic styles were promoted in specialty magazines and shops. The cosmopolitan cachet of an alternative fashion system tied to a proud, ascendant global *ummah* [community] added to its allure. Nancy Smith-Hefner has found that from fewer than 3% of middle-class female university students who chose to wear *jilbabs* [long, loose-fitting garments] on the Gadjah Mada University campus in the late 1970s, now over 60% do. Johan Lindquist has argued that among working-class migrants to the island of Batam, an Indonesian island bordering Singapore and the site of considerable offshore production, adoption of Islamic piety, partly through dress but also through other forms of devotion, has mitigated the sense of failure and degeneracy that marks the island. Movement through public space on the island has become a far more dangerous undertaking than in most other Indonesian cities. For young women who feel their journey to a distant location in pursuit of economic and personal advancement has not succeeded, vigilant attention to their religious purity can be comforting, especially if it protects them from accusations of immorality or sex work. As a result, Batam has one of the highest percentages of women who wear *jilbabs* in the country.

However, women who don such clothing yet who are judged to not take the garments' assumed essence seriously can come in for critique. Both Smith-Hefner and Lindquist show that while the adoption of *jilbabs* may make a woman feel some pride in her modern and stylish identity, or feel safe in a morally fraught and violent environment, its meanings are by no means fixed but rather are importantly dependent upon those who don and observe the garments in use. Both working and middle-class women who choose forms of Islamic dress are scrutinized for their choices and may be held to account by strangers for their public declaration of an Islamic identity. Any behavior contrary to the particular message the garments are thought to make can be policed. Batam women in *jilbabs* can be accused of using *jilbabs* strategically to conceal their true identities as prostitutes, while those who seek gynecological advice may be refused care on the grounds that pious women have no legitimate need for services only necessary for the sexually active. Similarly, women in Yogyakarta out in public after evening prayers may be reprimanded by self-appointed morality squads who argue that a key reason they must monitor the behavior of women in *busana Muslim* stems from the fact that the dress style has become so fashionable that women adopt it without making the corresponding personal and religious transformation. The allure of the commodity, in this logic, tempts women to make primarily consumer rather than religious choices, suggesting that the two qualities must be mutually exclusive. To quote a recent article, "women who wear *chadar* [a full-length open cloak] get called fanatics, while women at the other end of the spectrum come in for criticism as hypocrites."

Busana Muslim As One of Several Fashion Choices

The various dimensions of *Islami* dress, the rewards and risks of adopting it, are apparent in the experience of Ibu Evi. Known as a woman of impeccable religious credentials in Yogyakarta, Ibu Evi is regarded as a public figure of both excellent taste and piety. During the late 1990s, after making the *hajj*, Evi found herself increasingly pressured by men and women in her social class and religious circles to adopt *busana Muslim*. While she would occasionally do so for specific events, she generally ignored that pressure in favor of smart business dress. She insisted confidently to those who asked that she and God knew the state of her faith and that she did not feel it necessary to express that publicly. However, eight years later she now wears at least head covering and often full *busana Muslim* close to 30% of the time, she estimates. Several reasons have motivated this change. First, she acknowledges that more and more events that did not require Islamic dress in the past now do. Second, she finds the styles much more attractive and diverse than in the past and she no longer feels that dressing in a publicly Islamic way necessarily means dressing down or letting her beauty standards slip. Finally, and perhaps most importantly, she makes a point of appearing at events in unpredictable dress, sometimes in *busana Muslim* and other times not. Knowing that many people follow her dress and religious cues, she feels it is important for observers to recognize that she considers *busana Muslim* one of a variety of styles she inhabits, and that her piety is not directly linked to her dress. If *Islami* styles have become common, then she can wear *busana Muslim* intermittently, unlike in the past when the general sentiment was that the decision had to be total. That flexibility has been important for Evi, who enjoys playing with colors and styles in *busana Muslim*, but just as much enjoys having people know that she moves among dress types easily without diminishing her sense of devotion.

Women's Fashion Magazines Started Featuring More *Busana Muslim*

The increased visibility of *Islami* styles is also evident in the variety of urban, elite women's magazines such as *Femina*, the oldest and flagship journal of a now crowded market of nearly fifteen. *Femina*'s editors have consistently positioned their content and photo styles squarely in the voice of the intimate but superior older sister. Established in 1972 by a small group of prominent Jakarta businesswomen and modeled on a variety of American women's magazines, *Femina* established a hallmark mix of articles on marital advice, career advice, and cooking, decorating, and fashion tips. Readers are informed of fashion trends, both national and international, through photography spreads that frequently feature Indonesian designers few readers can afford. Photo spreads positioned fashion as thrilling and consumption as pleasurable, through instructional categories of career dress, neo-traditional styles, and more playful and bare styles, each positioned as equal choices from which a savvy dresser might select.

Rather than seeming a biting social critique, or feeling foreign, busana Muslim *had come to feel more like an unsurprising consumer choice among an array of dress styles for young women.*

In spite of this winning formula, by the mid-1990s editors told me they began to receive pleading and sometimes demanding letters from readers asking why Islamic fashions were not featured in these weekly spreads. Instead, Islamic fashions were only included in the magazine during the annual holiday periods of Idul Fitri and Ramadan and were often much more luxurious than would be appropriate for everyday wear. Indeed, such images frequently featured male models dressed in garb that clearly would only be worn for special religious occasions. Letter writers complained that the editors were forcing them to think up everyday fashionable Islamic looks on their own, without the trusted sisterly guidance they had come to rely on from the magazine. They argued that since they had taken up *busana Muslim* they could no longer see themselves reflected in the pages of the magazine and felt left out of the national fashion scene. Deploying the discursive authority of both consumption and of Islam, their requests for greater inclusion were voiced through the language of consumer choice. They framed their entitlement for equal coverage in the fashion press as a right due to them as consumers with the same funds and desire to spend in pursuit of identity as any other reader. As consumers who had made a personal and religious choice as individuals, they nonetheless took offense that this decision should be perceived as synonymous with taking no interest in looking attractive or being modern.

Editors explained to me that these letters forced them, in a sort of market-oriented, customer-knows-best way, into adjusting their content, moving ultimately to commission and running regular photo spreads that show women actively pursuing attractive, professional, and current lifestyles while dressed in *busana Muslim*. These run at least once a month and feature the work of a growing group of explicitly *Islami* designers, some of whose work is significantly more expensive than other local fashions featured in the magazine, but whose work is carefully presented as equal in style and sophistication to any other fashions in the magazine. Yet some editors also confessed that these letters had slightly irritated them. Considering that the editors fully considered themselves devout and faithful Muslims, having readers suggest that they were poor leaders and perhaps poor Muslims inverted the power relationship that the magazine had with its readers. Significantly, the way in which the editors could mitigate this accusation and reclaim the magazine's voice of authority was to turn *busana Muslim* into fashion, for that was the terrain of their expertise. Photo spreads that placed a woman in *busana Muslim* in the same frame as a woman in generic corporate dress suggested that either option was equally fashionable and that selecting between the two was primarily a consumer and aesthetic choice, rather than a political or religious practice. In a way, then, the commodification and fashioning of *busana*

The Islamic World Adopts Various Items of Ethnic Dress

Garments like the *kaftan* and *salwaar kamiz*—originally items of ethnic dress that were associated with a particular country or group of people—have now spread throughout the Islamic world. Since the 1980s, a number of factors have contributed to increasing interaction between Muslims from different countries. Petrodollars pay for labor migration to the Middle East and fund scholarships for students from Africa and Southeast Asia to attend universities in Saudi Arabia. Satellite television stations like Al Jazeera and Al Arabiya—owned and run by Muslims—offer an alternative to CNN and the BBC. Web sites and online stores display Islamic fashions, but they also offer Muslims living in areas where they are not in a majority the chance to have the same kinds of clothing and dress practices as those who live in the *Dar al-Islam* (the Islamic world). Styles of dress from Jordan and Turkey have appeared as fashions among Somalis in the United States, crossing the boundaries of ethnic groups and nations. Although Islamic fashions might appear and even be discussed as traditions, many of these are not just "ethnic" but do appeal to a global audience.

Heather Marie Akou,
"Building a New 'World Fashion': Islamic Dress in the Twenty-First Century,"
Fashion Theory: The Journal of Body, Dress & Culture, *2007.*

Muslim in the fashion press appeared to soften the more politically sharp critique that the editors perceived in these letters.

Two new magazines now dominate the Islamic women's market, *Noor* and *Ummi*. Patterned almost identically on magazines such as *Femina*, with advice columns, fashion spreads, recipes, and interior design, *Noor* magazine takes a sisterly tone in sharing with readers tips on how to dress piously and fashionably. An important emphasis is on translation, offering equivalent Islamic gestures or styles for everyday activities that a modern pious woman might require, yet assume that most readers nonetheless wish to be attractive and "chic." Columns address how to handle greetings with men, how to deal with office politics, and frequent letters from readers who identify as having just begun to wear *busana Muslim*, seeking a way to convert their personal aesthetic into *Islami* style. Editors assume the one factor common to their readership is an explicitly Islamic identity, but generally assume that readers are active in the public sphere, either as professionals or as social volunteers. The expertise navigates local and global differences, positioning moral advice and Islamic fashion as global, rooted in the international makeup of the *ummah* and the universal truth of the Koran and hadith [records of the sayings of Muhammad], while local ethnic traditions provide colorful accents and unique touches, adding authenticity and national pride. In all these magazines, *Femina*, *Ummi*, and *Noor*, Islamic fashions bear little trace of their elite social structure, suggesting that what would for many women involve a significant jump in socioeconomic position, i.e., the complete restructuring of a wardrobe and perhaps decreased work outside the home, is primarily a personal choice of religious devotion available to any woman who is so called.

Some Young Students Consider Western Dress Too Secular

A second example further elucidates this turn towards more visible public use of Islamic dress in contemporary Java [an island of Indonesia]. In the decade prior to the 1997–8 economic crisis a small industry of instructional femininity courses flourished in many Javanese cities, as well as on Sumatra and Bali. The course I studied was offered by a small private business college run by a modernist Islamic institute in a prestigious part of Yogyakarta. Like many such colleges, it offers short courses on business presentation, public relations techniques and public speaking, in addition to a course called "Personal Development" (*Pengembangan Pribadi*). I use the term femininity course to describe these courses because, although it is not based on the Indonesian term for the course, it conveys the gender-specific content of the course. Goals for most students included career and social advancement, which they couched in terms of desire for increased self-esteem, the sort of self-mastery and sense of identity that was appealing at a time of social flux (*percaya diri* or literally "belief in oneself"). Instructors in the course measured student self-esteem through vocal and carriage skills. Particular emphasis was placed on appropriating fashions and personal skills from expert sources (such as local and foreign magazines, television, and motivational philosophies such as Stephen Covey's) in ways consistent with what was considered Indonesian and feminine. The course I studied had been open for five years, although similar courses had been successfully operating in the capital city Jakarta since 1982. Instructors emphasized that students should attempt to minimize their provincial tastes through selecting styles of hair, dress, and comportment that were appropriate to their future employment and their roles as modern Indonesian women. By 2000–1, a significant point of tension between students and instructors centered on their often generational differences in interpreting Islam. Instructors in the course, who viewed themselves as faithful Muslims and in many cases understood their role in the course with an almost missionary-style zeal, nonetheless increasingly found themselves faced with students who had chosen clothing styles associated with pious Islamic practice and who saw themselves as therefore more devout than instructors whose expertise they paid handsomely to acquire.

Many course participants, when asked by instructors about their decision to wear *busana Muslim*, said they did so out of a desire to critique corrupt representations of femininity and because the Koran states a woman must cover in public. To these students, Western-style dress was corrupt, not because it came from some place called the "West," but because it had become the style of an older generation of Indonesian women whom they felt had embraced a secular pursuit of personal enrichment, a generation that represented course instructors. Differing interpretations of Islam were therefore a source of polite negotiation between instructors and students in the course. The decision to wear a *jilbab* was neither discouraged nor encouraged by the instructors. Students frequently asked etiquette questions on how to handle interactions between the sexes outside the home. Such interactions were addressed in the basic course content, but did include Islamically specific variations for potentially awkward situations such as introductions or work-related dinner engagements between men and women. Instructors sometimes perceived students' questions around issues of Muslim clothing and manners as a subtle critique of an instructor's choice not to participate in such scrupulous self-monitoring. Like *Femina*'s editors, these instructors were well-respected, religiously devout leaders who could become frustrated at subtle hints of their laxity. Students who chose to wear the *jilbab* were therefore carefully informed that their decisions would entail additional steps of self-maintenance, including extra salon trips and hair treatments to manage skin and hair subjected to the effects of heat and damp fabric on the skin. On occasion, one instructor would remind students that because *busana Muslim* eschewed body-conscious cuts, women might become lazy about maintaining an attractive figure and allow their loose clothing to hide an overweight body. Another instructor known as a respected *hajji* [elder] would warmly but pointedly joke with students that if the point of a *jilbab* was to cover the head, but not to diminish one's persona as a woman of good taste, then a wig should be an equivalent option. Yet the instructors and students still shared a commitment to personal self-transformation through self-discipline, a theme that generally overcame the particular details of how to achieve that transformation.

In the examples I have described, younger, more self-consciously styled women both critiqued their parents' generation for its participation in the New Order's morally bankrupt social and political project, yet they also asked of women of that generation that their own religious choices be acknowledged and addressed as more than a political act, but also as an attractive and expressive fashion choice.

Some Muslim Women Are Able to Feel Both Pious and Fashionable

In the examples I have described, younger, more self-consciously styled women both critiqued their parents' generation for its participation in the New Order's morally bankrupt social and political project, yet they also asked of women of that generation that their own religious choices be acknowledged and addressed as more than a political act, but also as an attractive and expressive fashion choice. They demanded to be "seen" as fashionable, and they were at the vanguard of a now booming and ubiquitous Islamic fashion industry in Indonesia, from lipsticks to socks to gloves to brightly colored fabric tunics and scarves. Given the degree to which this industry has taken off since the end of the New Order, when Islamic identity has now become more available and less risky as well as potentially more comforting given the social uncertainties surrounding a state of apparently unending crisis, it would be tempting to argue that these styles have been reduced, through their commodification, to merely that: style, bereft of any original political potency or personal piety. Such an assumption requires that we reduce the possibilities in piety or consumption to mutually exclusive and contradictory analytical categories. Yet the layers of complex readings and misreadings from the examples offered in this [viewpoint] suggest that *busana Muslim* cannot be reduced to a singular meaning, for wearers or observers. Perhaps most compelling, those who see the least contradiction are those who inhabit the position of pious consumers, women who write to magazines or take femininity courses as confident buyers of an attractive, stylish, pious look. While their letters, or their fashions, may be interpreted differently from what they intend, at least for a moment, they take inspiration and satisfaction from being simultaneously pious and fashionable.

Viewpoint 3

Some British Muslims Find the Islamic Burqa to Be Abhorrent

Yasmin Alibhai-Brown

Yasmin Alibhai-Brown is a Muslim woman living in Great Britain. She believes strongly that Muslim women should not wear the burqa, or Islamic veil. In the following viewpoint, Alibhai-Brown states the religious and political reasons she believes as she does.

As you read, consider the following questions:

1. What does Alibhai-Brown say is the true injunction for all Muslims, instead of wearing the veil?
2. As quoted by Alibhai-Brown, why does Rahila Gupta say the veil is soaked in blood?
3. Why does the author say that faces should be unveiled?

I am a Shia Muslim and I abhor the *burqa*. I am offended by the unchallenged presumption that women covering their heads and bodies and now faces are more pious and true than am I.

Islam in all its diverse forms entitles believers to a personal relationship with Allah—it cuts out middlemen, one reason its appeal extended to so many across the world. You can seek advice from learned scholars and imams, but they

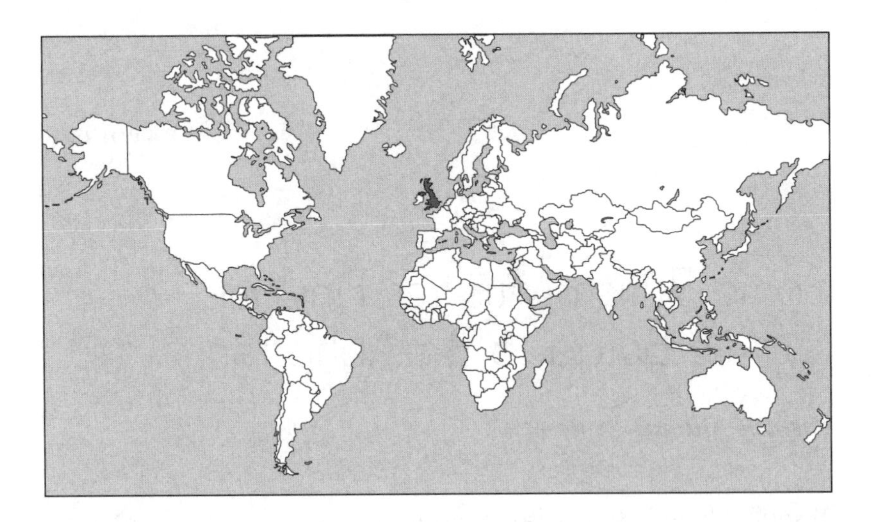

cannot come between your faith and the light of God. Today control freaks who claim they have a special line to the Almighty have turned our world dark. Neo-conservative Islamic codes spread like swine flu, an infection few seem able to resist.

The disease is progressive. It started 20 years ago with the *hijab*, donned then as a defiant symbol of identity, now a conscript's uniform. Then came the *jilbab*, the cloak, fought over in courts when schoolgirls were manipulated into claiming it as an essential Islamic garment. If so, hell awaits the female leaders of Pakistan and Bangladesh.

Soon, children as young as four were kitted up in cloaks and head scarves ("so they get used to it, and then later wear the full thing," said a teacher to me who works at a Muslim girls' school) and now for the graduation gown, a full *burqa*, preferably with dark glasses.

White liberals frame this sinister development in terms of free choice and tolerance. Some write letters to this paper: What is the problem? It is all part of the rich diversity of our nation. They can rise to this challenge, show they are superhuman when it comes to liberty and forbearance.

They might not be quite so sanguine if their own daughters decided to be fully veiled or their sons became fanatic Islamicists and imposed *purdah* in the family. Such converts are springing up in Muslim families all over the land. Veils predate Islam and were never an injunction (modesty of attire for men and women is). Cultural protectionism has long been extended to those who came from old colonies, in part to atone for imperial hauteur. Redress was necessary then, not now.

Muslim women who show their hair are becoming endangered species.

What about legitimate fears that to criticise vulnerable ethnic and racial groups validates the racism they face? Racism is an evil but should never be used as an alibi to acquit oppressions within black and Asian or religious communities. That cry was used to deter us from exposing forced marriages and dowry deaths and black-upon-black violence.

Right-wing think tanks and President Sarkozy of France scapegoat Muslims for political gain and British fascists have turned self-inflicted "ethnic" wounds into scarlet propaganda. They do what they always have done. Self-censorship will not stop them but it does stop us from dealing with homegrown problems or articulating objections to reactionary life choices like the *burqa*. Muslim women who show their hair are becoming an endangered species. We must fight back. Our covered-up sisters do not understand history, politics, struggles, their faith or equality. As Rahila Gupta, campaigner against domestic violence, writes: "This is a cloth that comes soaked in blood. We cannot debate the *burqa* or the *hijab* without reference to women in Iran, Afghanistan or Saudi Arabia where the wearing of it is heavily policed and any slippages are met with violence." What happened to solidarity?

"Underneath, I'm wearing designer jeans, too," cartoon by Harley Schwadron, www.CartoonStock.com. Copyright © Harley Schwadron. Reproduction rights obtainable from www.CartoonStock.com.

Violent enforcement is evident in Britain too. A fully veiled young chemistry graduate once came to my home, her body covered in cuts, tears, bites, bruises, all happily hidden from view. Security and social cohesion are all threatened by this trend—which is growing exponentially.

As for the pathetic excuse that covering up protects women from male lasciviousness—it hasn't stopped rapists in the most conservative Muslim nations. And what a slur on decent Muslim men, portrayed as sexual predators who cannot look upon a woman without wanting her.

We communicate with each other with our faces. To deny that interaction is to deny our shared humanity. Unreasonable community or nationalistic expectations disconnect essential bonds. Governments should not accommodate such demands.

Naturists can't parade on the streets, go to school or take up jobs unless they cover their nakedness. Why should *burqaed* women get special consideration?

Their veils are walls, keeping them in and us out. We need an urgent, open conversation on this issue—which divides the Muslim intelligentsia as much as the nation. Our social environment, fragile and precious, matters more than choice and custom should to British Muslims. If we don't compromise for the greater good, the future looks only more bitter and bleak. Saying so doesn't make me the enemy of my people.

Viewpoint 4

Women in India Are Intimately Connected to Their Saris

Mukulika Banerjee and Daniel Miller

Mukulika Banerjee and Daniel Miller are professors of anthropology at University College in London. In the following viewpoint, they discuss the sari, a traditional garment from India that consists of a single long strip of cloth wrapped around the body. They describe the sensations of wearing a sari and the relationship that develops between a woman and the garment.

As you read, consider the following questions:

1. Why do the authors say the navel is the focal pivot of the security of the sari?
2. In the constant battle to make her "second skin" obey her will, what do the authors say the woman gets for her victory?
3. How do the authors compare an urban middle-class woman's feelings about her sari to those of a villager?

The Feel of the Sari

Clothes are among our most personal possessions. They are the main medium between our sense of our bodies and our sense of the external world. The sensual qualities of the sari,

Mukulika Banerjee and Daniel Miller, *The Sari*, London, United Kingdom: Berg, 2003, pp. 24–29.

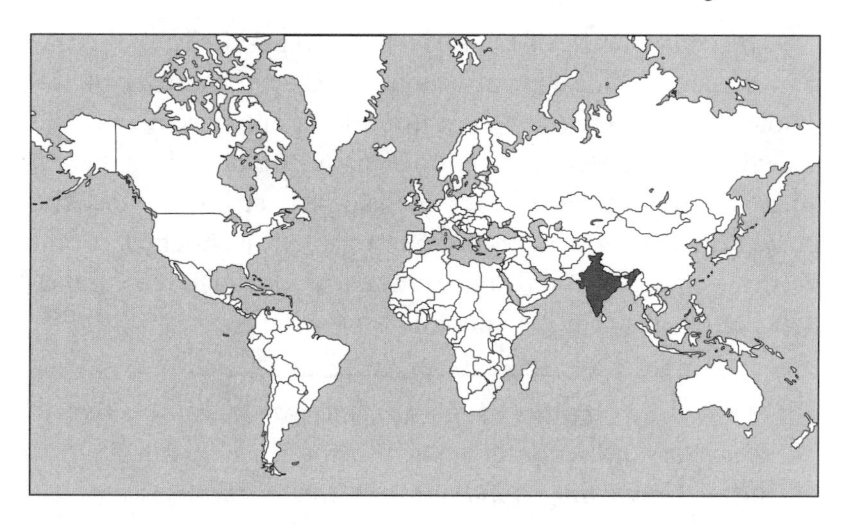

the way it feels on the skin, profoundly affects womens' experience of the garment as something simultaneously part of them yet outside of them.

To wear clothing is to be subject to different sensations with varying intensities, as we are conscious of only certain points of contact between flesh and cloth. In the now widespread Nivi style, the sari is draped from right to left, passing over the lower body twice—the second time in a cluster of fan-shaped pleats—and the upper body once. The pallu, the free end of the sari, falls over the left shoulder down to the waist. Given the asymmetry of the sari, no sensation in one part of the body is repeated in any other. The right leg does not feel like the mirror of the left. The two shoulders and the two breasts are touched by the garment in quite different ways. The right shoulder can remain untouched by the sari, while the left bears the weight of the pallu. The right breast feels the pressure of the pleats of the pallu pulled across the bosom, whereas the left one feels strangely exposed, covered from the front but visible from the side. The right side of the waist is hot from the pleats passing over it, but the left side is uncovered and cool.

The centre point of the sari—the navel—carries the sensation of being a focal pivot around which the security of the whole garment revolves. Here the pleats are tucked into the drawstring of the petticoat. About a yard of cloth is gathered, with a good five inches tucked inside the string, against the belly. This causes perspiration, and a *zari* or starched cotton border may scratch, but these sensations also give reassurance that the pleats are not spilling out.

The sensual qualities of the sari, the way it feels on the skin profoundly affects womens' experience of the garment as something simultaneously part of them yet outside of them.

The thighs help define the graceful folds of the pleats that fan out from between the legs. Here again the sensations are asymmetrical. The pleats often lie from right to left in such a way that the first pleat rests on the right leg while the last pleat rests against the left leg. It is how one holds the right leg and knee that defines the shape of the pleats, but it is from the left leg that the sari curves from mid-thigh around towards the back of the body, resting in folds on the back of one's waist to then be brought around from the right side as the pallu. So the curve of a woman's hip and waist is accentuated on the left side. A slight bend at the knee can create a horizontal break in the vertical folds of the sari, giving a woman a more feminine and statuesque look. The ankles always feel slightly crowded as the gathers of the folds of the sari rest against them, their touch made heavier by the 'fall'.

When walking, the right leg determines the length of the stride, which is kept in check by the warning tension at the ankle when the stride is too long for the sari. The left leg needs to move a little bit out and forward so as not to trap the pleats between the knees. The pallu may slide off with the movement, in which case the right arm comes up to restore it to the left shoulder, but carefully so as not to crush the cloth. After a few strides the sari may slip down from the left waist, and the left arm needs to pull it back up in order to retain the fan shape of the pleats.

As they sit down, women invariably check that the pallu has not slipped from covering the right breast, and that the waist is not too exposed by the folding of the torso. The folding of the body upon sitting down in a rickshaw or a car tends also to crush the sari in front and threatens the sequence of the pleats. A series of adjustments is required to even out the part of the pallu which is visible in the front; the pleats need to be rearranged to help them retain their order, and the pallu needs to be freed from being trapped beneath the bottom.

Different sorts of weather create their own sensations and problems. The perspiration that accumulates where the sari is tucked in or densely bunched is mainly unseen. Indeed, the perspiration running down the legs meets the air circulating there, creating a pleasurable cooling sensation. When the waist becomes too damp and itchy, a woman can push the petticoat string to a fresh patch of skin on the waist. In wet weather the bottom of the sari tends to be soaked first, making it heavy and pulling the whole garment downwards. The sari loses its shape and is harder to control or feel comfortable in. A wet sari also clings to the body at various points, accentuating curves and dips of its own accord, rather than as intended by the wearer.

For most women today, the relationship between the sari and the body is mediated by the presence of undergarments.

Thinking of the sari as an unstitched garment, we might imagine it as particularly loose and comfortable. This may well have been the experience of women in the past, and indeed for some older women in rural areas today. But elsewhere the number of women who wear only a single unstitched piece of cloth is rapidly diminishing, and for the rest the desire to look modern involves tightly fitted stitched accompanying garments which are the very opposite of loose comfort. As a thirty-something advertising executive from Mumbai commented:

> The petticoat and the fitting of the blouse has really to be tight. A thousand years ago, when the sari evolved, nobody wore a petticoat. It was just one piece of clothing and even the blouse was worn tied around, like a bustier. So it was perfect for the tropics. But the way we wear it today, thanks to the missionaries, is horrible.

The blouse is tight, has sleeves of varying lengths and ends near the waist. The petticoat is a full-length skirt, tied at the waist with a drawstring. The sari is draped over these accessories. Many women who prefer to wear a shalwar kamiz cite its advantage as being loose-fitting compared to the tight-fitting sari blouse.

The sari wearer sees herself as engaged in a constant battle to make her 'second skin', that six yard piece of rectangular cloth, move, drape, sit, fold, pleat and swirl in a manner obedient to her will. What victory gives her, however, is a remarkable flexibility to accentuate, moderate or even hide features of her body. But this requires a constant, though unconscious, responsiveness to the way the sari moves with every gesture that she makes. This is in striking contrast to stitched clothing, which once put on in the morning is largely taken for granted for the rest of the day. The sari forces a continued engagement, a conversation, between a woman and her garment.

This conversation includes a subtle alternation between actions that become almost unconscious or automatic, and others that are highly self-conscious. This word is particularly appropriate, since an effect of the sari is often to give wearers a heightened sense of themselves. Recall how Mina, the neophyte sari wearer, lives in constant fear of embarrassment even within her home. She can hardly sleep because she is so afraid that loss of consciousness will lead to her head or knees being

An Indian Woman Explains How She Adds Adornments to Her Sari

Mukta [Tripathi, an Indian woman] believes that beauty results from an artful assemblage created on the body. Jewelry and the body must match each other; she sees them as interdependent. But individual items of adornment must also suit each other, coming together in an appealing way. While she conforms to the norms of acceptable ensemble, Mukta adds a top layer, rich with personal taste. Most married women in India wear a sari with gold jewelry, especially when they are attending a social function. Mukta is no exception, but instead of simply matching the attire (sari) with the jewelry (gold), she matches the color and material of the sari with the material and style of the jewelry, taking the daily task one step further. I asked Mukta to describe one of these successful combinations. She said, "For example, if there is a pink color sari, with that I will wear all pearl jewelry. Like a pink color or yellow color sari—with these, I usually tend to wear pearl sets. That's what looks good, on pink."

Pravina Shukla,
The Grace of Four Moons.
Bloomington, IN: Indiana University Press, 2008, p. 266.

uncovered, and as a result she feels stifled in the summer nights. Her worry about the sari falling off leads her to tie her petticoat string so tightly that the doctor is convinced she will harm the baby growing inside her. Yet all the while she is also developing a familiarity with the garment, such that some of her actions become increasingly natural and automatic and she loses awareness that she is inhabiting the sari and its requirements. This process culminates symbolically in the moment when she criticises as 'disrespectful' a woman who has worn a suit rather than a sari during a Bengali festival.

Such self-consciousness is always experienced in the light of particular cultural ideals and fear of social disdain. An urban middle-class woman may strongly believe that the sari can and should command a particular grace or elegance, and be driven to strive to live up to this image of what we shall call the 'elevated sari'. A villager, in contrast, may be self-conscious about different aspects of her clothing: How can she walk in order best to prevent her sari's rents and faded patches from showing? What both women are likely to hold in common, however, is the continued and powerful belief in the special capacity of the sari to make a body more beautiful and womanly than any other garment.

This degree of intimacy in the relationship between wearer and sari may lead to a sense of the sari itself as animated: as having, in a metaphorical sense, a life of its own. This emerges even in the most unlikely areas, such as the maintenance of cleaning, starching and pressing. Starching, for example, may in its own way be expressive of the intimate relationship between the sari and its wearer. A well-starched sari may look more beautiful and its pleats will stay in place, but it has none of the softness that makes well-worn unstarched cotton such a pleasure on the skin. As an old (and on that day frail) village woman told us:

> Now I have a fever and don't feel good so I don't feel like wearing my new sari which I just received yesterday at this wedding I sang at. This old one feels much better as it is soft and old, and it's light. In general it is better to wear old saris when doing housework since it is soft and you know where it is. A new one is crisp and you can't control it and tie it around your waist, and then it might catch fire in front of the hearth.

This leads to a sense that the sari has a life that can be extended by proper starching: 'especially when they wore thin, I used to starch them lightly and then have them ironed before putting them away'. Further, the substance that gives them more life, the starch itself, is traditionally the water used for boiling rice. This becomes in turn a metaphor about feeding a sari. A villager notes:

> If I could eat grapes and fruit then would I look like this, wasted and thin? I would have more blood in my body. But if I only eat stale rice, how can I have blood in my body? All the blood will dry up. It's the same with a sari.

This relationship becomes particularly poignant under conditions of poverty when rice is synonymous with food and survival. One of the enduring images of the Bengal Famine of 1943 is that of starving and desperate people drinking the waste starch water from wealthier homes. Feeding a sari with the rice water that was once needed for personal survival contributes to this sense that the sari itself has an animate element, which the owner will seek to keep alive as long as possible. From this develops broader metaphors linking the life of a person and her sari. Sixty-year-old Asma, when asked whether she still had her wedding saris, laughed, saying: 'How can I still have them? They have torn and disappeared years ago. Look at the way a person ages and gets old; how can a sari remain for so long?' . . .

Periodical Bibliography

The following articles have been selected to supplement the diverse views presented in this chapter.

Amany Abdel-Moneim	"Move Over, Barbie," *Al-Ahram Weekly* (Cairo, Egypt), June 12, 2006.
Heather Marie Akou	"Building a New 'World Fashion': Islamic Dress in the Twenty-First Century," *Fashion Theory: The Journal of Dress, Body & Culture*, December 2007.
Judy Bachrach	"The French Connection. (French Women, Beauty, and Fashion)," *Allure*, July 1, 2005.
Sisylia Octavia Candra	"Traditional Fashions of Indonesia," *ChildArt*, January–March 2006.
Amelia Gentleman	"Don't Tell Liz, but the Sari's So Out," *Observer* (UK), April 29, 2005.
Elisabeth Hackspiel	"Modernity and Tradition in a Global World: Fashion in Africa," *African Arts*, Summer 2008.
Sarah Raper Larenaudie	"Under Cover," *Time*, February 21, 2008.
Annelies Moors and Emma Tarlo	"Fashionable Muslims: Notions of Self, Religion, and Society in San'a," *Fashion Theory: The Journal of Dress, Body & Culture*, June 2007.
Bronwyn Winter	"The Great Hijab Coverup," *Off Our Backs*, vol. 36, no. 3, 2006.
LI Yongyan	"A Study on the Application of Elements of Ethnic Dress in Modern Fashion Design," *Canadian Social Science*, April 2009.

For Further Discussion

Chapter 1

1. Lars Svendsen contends that there are no universal ideals of beauty. Do you agree or disagree? Why or why not?
2. What factors do you think affect how standards of beauty are determined in different parts of the world? Cite specific examples from the viewpoints to bolster your argument.

Chapter 2

1. After reading the viewpoints in this chapter, what relationship do you see between ideal body image and self-esteem?

Chapter 3

1. Compare tribal methods of body enhancement such as body painting with more modern methods such as skin lightening and cosmetic surgery. In what ways are they similar? In what ways are they different?

Chapter 4

1. How does ethnic dress help a cultural group identify itself and separate itself from the outside world?
2. Is exposure to fashion of other cultures beneficial? Draw from the viewpoints in Chapter 4 to explain your answer.

Organizations to Contact

The editors have compiled the following list of organizations concerned with the issues debated in this book. The descriptions are derived from materials provided by the organizations. All have publications or information available for interested readers. The list was compiled on the date of publication of the present volume; the information provided here may change. Be aware that many organizations take several weeks or longer to respond to inquiries, so allow as much time as possible.

Academy for Eating Disorders (AED)
111 Deer Lake Road, Suite 100, Deerfield, IL 60015
(847) 498-4274 • fax: (847) 480-9282
e-mail: info@aedweb.org
Web site: www.aedweb.org

Headquartered in Illinois, the Academy for Eating Disorders (AED) is an international organization for eating disorder treatment, research, and education. It provides professional training and education; encourages new developments in eating disorders research, prevention, and clinical treatments; and is an international source for state-of-the-art information in the field of eating disorders. The AED upholds that the beauty and fashion industries should promote a healthy body image and address eating disorders within the modeling profession.

Africa Regional Sexuality Resource Centre (ARSRC)
PO Box 803, Yaba, Lagos
Nigeria
234-1-7919307 • fax: 234-1-3425470
e-mail: info@arsrc.org
Web site: www.arsrc.org

The Africa Regional Sexuality Resource Centre (ARSRC), established in 2003, is part of a Ford Foundation five-year grant-making initiative, "Global Dialogue of Sexual Health and Well

Being" aimed at giving visibility, depth and legitimacy to the field of sexuality. The goal of the ARSRC is to promote more informed and affirming public dialogue on human sexuality and to contribute to positive changes in the emerging field of sexuality in Africa by creating mechanisms for learning at the regional level. The organization's publications, available online, include articles on body image in Africa.

American Psychological Association (APA)
750 First Street NE, Washington, DC 20002-4242
(800) 374-2721
Web site: www.apa.org

Based in Washington, D.C., the American Psychological Association (APA) is a scientific and professional organization that represents psychology in the United States. With 150,000 members, APA is the largest association of psychologists worldwide. It publishes articles and reports on beauty, cosmetic surgery, and other related topics in its numerous journals, and its books include *The Psychology of Beauty* and *Body Image, Eating Disorders, and Obesity in Youth*. Many of the organization's articles can be read online through the APA Web site.

American Society of Plastic Surgeons (ASPS)
444 E. Algonquin Road, Arlington Heights, IL 60005
(847) 228-9900
Web site: www.plasticsurgery.org

The American Society of Plastic Surgeons (ASPS) is the largest plastic surgery specialty organization in the world. Established in 1931, it offers patients and consumers information on cosmetic and reconstructive surgery procedures, an online database of plastic surgery statistics, and technology briefs on the latest developments and advances in the field.

Color Foundation
e-mail: info@colorfoundation.org
Web site: www.colorfoundation.org

The Color Foundation, an independent international organization, furthers activities on biological and social aspects of skin color to improve relations between people worldwide. The organization focuses on a multitude of issues including the evolution of skin color and the history of free or forced migration of people in order to understand the past and present attitude toward skin color. Information on skin color can be found on Color Foundation's Web site and blog.

Council of Fashion Designers of America (CFDA)
1412 Broadway, Suite 2006, New York, NY 10018
Web site: www.cfda.com

The Council of Fashion Designers of America (CFDA) is a not-for-profit trade association of more than 350 of America's foremost fashion and accessory designers. Founded in 1962, the CFDA continues to advance the status of fashion design as a branch of American art and culture, to raise its artistic and professional standards, to define a code of ethical practices of mutual benefit in public and trade relations, and to promote appreciation of the fashion arts through leadership in quality and aesthetic discernment. CFDA's annual report, available on its Web site, provides an overview of current American fashion trends.

Environmental Working Group (EWG)
1436 U Street NW, Suite 100, Washington, DC 20009
(202) 667-6982
Web sites: www.ewg.org

Environmental Working Group is a nonprofit organization whose mission is to use the power of public information to protect public health and the environment. EWG's Skin Deep, launched in 2004, is an online safety guide for more than fifty thousand cosmetics and personal care products.

Personal Care Products Council (PCPC)
1101 Seventeenth Street NW, Suite 300
Washington, DC 20036-4702

(202) 331-1770 • fax: (202) 331-1969
Web site: www.personalcarecouncil.org

Personal Care Products Council, or PCPC (formerly the Cosmetic, Toiletry and Fragrance Association), is a national trade association for the cosmetic and personal care products industry and represents the most innovative names in beauty today. For more than six hundred member companies, the council is the voice on scientific, legal, regulatory, legislative, and international issues for the personal care products industry. PCPC also sponsors a Web site for consumers, www.cosmeticsinfo.org, which contains information about the safety, testing, and regulation of cosmetics and personal care products and their ingredients.

United Nations Educational, Scientific and Cultural Organization (UNESCO)
7, Place de Fontenoy 75352, Paris 07 SP
France
+33 (0)1 45 68 10 00 • fax: +33 (0)1 45 67 16 90
e-mail: bpi@unesco.org
Web site: www.unesco.org

The United Nations Educational, Scientific and Cultural Organization (UNESCO) works to create the conditions for dialogue among civilizations, cultures, and peoples, based upon respect for commonly shared values. Through this dialogue, UNESCO strives to help the world to achieve global visions of sustainable development, encompassing observance of human rights, mutual respect, and the alleviation of poverty, all of which are at the heart of UNESCO's mission and activities.

U.S. Food and Drug Administration (FDA)
10903 New Hampshire Avenue, Silver Spring, MD 20993
(888) INFO-FDA (463-6332)
Web site: www.fda.gov

The U.S. Food and Drug Administration (FDA) is an agency within the U.S. Department of Health and Human Services, one of the nation's oldest consumer protection agencies. The

FDA's mission is to promote and protect the public health by ensuring that safe and effective products reach the market; by monitoring products for continued safety after they are in use; and by helping the public get the accurate, science-based information needed to improve health. The FDA provides information on the ingredients and labeling of cosmetics and personal care products.

World Fashion Council (WFC)
24B Monroe Street, Norwalk, CT 06854
(203) 345-0030
e-mail: marc@worldfashioncouncll.org
Web site: www.worldfashioncouncil.org

The World Fashion Council (WFC), an organization supporting young designers, encourages innovation in design excellence in fashion and design education. The council raises industry standards for market forecasting and consulting, and it fosters the emergence of a network of fashion designers, fashion weeks, and fashion design associations throughout the world. The organization opens a cross-cultural exchange between fashion programs and young designers throughout the world and creates a central event that brings together young designers, the colleges and universities they attend, and top-tier fashion brands and professionals. WFC's Web site includes articles on world fashion.

Bibliography of Books

Nilda Callañaupa Alvarez — *Weaving in the Peruvian Highlands: Dreaming Patterns, Weaving Memories*. Cusco, Peru: Center de Textiles Traditionales del Cusco, 2007.

Patricia Rieff Anawalt — *The Worldwide History of Dress*. New York: Thames & Hudson, 2007.

John Armstrong — *The Secret Power of Beauty*. London: Allen Lane, 2004.

Ben Arogundade — *Black Beauty: A History and a Celebration*. New York: Thunder's Mouth Press, 2000.

Vandana Bhandari — *Costumes, Textiles and Jewellery of India: Traditions in Rajasthan*. New Delhi, India: Prakash Books India, 2004.

Peter Corrigan — *The Dressed Society: Clothing, the Body and Some Meanings of the World*. London: SAGE Publications, 2008.

Maxine Leeds Craig — *Ain't I a Beauty Queen?: Black Women, Beauty, and the Politics of Race*. Oxford, UK: Oxford University Press, 2002.

Rosemary Crill, Jennifer Wearden, and Verity Wilson — *World Dress Fashion in Detail*. London: V & A Publishing, 2009.

Mary Lynn Damhorst, Kimberly A. Miller, and Susan O. Michelman	*The Meanings of Dress*. New York: Fairchild Publications, 1999.
Jeanine Downie and Fran Cook-Bolden	*Beautiful Skin of Color: A Comprehensive Guide to Asian, Olive, and Dark Skin*. New York: Regan Books, 2004.
Eve Ensler	*The Good Body*. New York: Villard, 2004.
Samuel S. Epstein and Randall Fitzgerald	*Toxic Beauty: How Cosmetics and Personal Care Products Endanger Your Health . . . and What You Can Do About It*. Dallas, TX: BenBella Books, 2009.
Shari Graydon	*In Your Face: The Culture of Beauty and You*. Toronto: Annick Press, 2004.
Stephen Gundle	*Bellissima: Feminine Beauty and the Idea of Italy*. New Haven, CT: Yale University Press, 2007.
Ronald E. Hall	*Bleaching Beauty: Light Skin as a Filipina Ideal*. Quezon City, Philippines: Giraffe Books, 2006.
Jennifer Heath, ed.	*The Veil: Women Writers on Its History, Lore, and Politics*. Berkeley, CA: University of California Press, 2008.
Andrea M. Heckman	*Woven Stories: Andean Textiles and Rituals*. Albuquerque, NM: University of New Mexico Press, 2003.

Nina G. Jablonski	*Skin: A Natural History*. Berkeley, CA: University of California Press, 2006.
Paul Jobling	*Man Appeal: Advertising, Modernism and Men's Wear*. Oxford, UK: Berg, 2005.
Donald Clay Johnson and Helen Bradley Foster, eds.	*Dress Sense: Emotional and Sensory Experiences of the Body and Clothes*. New York: Berg, 2007.
Christian Joppke	*Veil: Mirror of Identity*. Cambridge, MA: Polity, 2009.
Rebecca Chiyoko King-O'Riain	*Pure Beauty: Judging Race in Japanese American Beauty Pageants*. Minneapolis, MN: University of Minnesota Press, 2006.
Lars F. Krutak	*The Tattooing Arts of Tribal Women*. London: Bennett & Bloom/Desert Hearts, 2007.
Claudia Malacrida and Jacqueline Low, eds.	*Sociology of the Body: A Reader*. Don Mills, Ontario: Oxford University Press, 2008.
Stacy Malkan	*Not Just a Pretty Face: The Ugly Side of the Beauty Industry*. Gabriola Island, BC: New Society Publishers, 2007.
Eugenia Paulicelli and Hazel Clark, eds.	*The Fabric of Cultures: Fashion, Identity, and Globalization*. London: Routledge, 2009.

Mina Roces and Louise Edwards, eds.	*The Politics of Dress in Asia and the Americas*. Portland, OR: Sussex Academic Press, 2007.
Ligaya Salazar, ed.	*Fashion v Sport*. London: V&A Publishing, 2008.
Hans Silvester	*Natural Fashion: Tribal Decoration from Africa*. London: Thames & Hudson, 2008.
Andy Sloss	*Celtic Tattoos*. London: Carlton Books Limited, 2007.
Viren Swami and Adrian Furnham, eds.	*The Body Beautiful: Evolutionary and Sociocultural Perspectives*. Basingstoke, UK: Palgrave Macmillan, 2007.
Shirley Anne Tate	*Black Beauty: Aesthetics, Stylization, Politics*. Farnham, Surrey, England: Ashgate, 2009.
Jacelyn Tay	*Makeup for Asian Women*. Singapore: Times Editions-Marshall Cavendish, 2005.
Gillian Vogelsang-Eastwood and Willem Vogelsang	*Covering the Moon: An Introduction to Middle Eastern Face Veils*. Leuven, Belgium: Peeters, 2008.
Elwood Watson and Darcy Martin, eds.	*"There She Is, Miss America": The Politics of Sex, Beauty, and Race in America's Most Famous Pageant*. New York: Palgrave Macmillan, 2004.
Linda Welters and Abby Lillethun, eds.	*The Fashion Reader*. New York: Berg, 2007.

Index

Geographic headings and page numbers in **boldface** refer to viewpoints about that country or region.

C

D

E

F

N

O

P

Q

R

S